The Memory of Water
&
Five Kinds of Silence

The Memory of Water
'Not many dramatists have as sharp an eye for the quirks of character as Stephenson, and still fewer are so adroit when it comes to turning comic dialogue' *The Times*

'Blessedly and mercurially funny . . . Stephenson, a mistress of comic anguish, is clearly a real find' *Guardian*

Five Kinds of Silence
Winner of the 1996 Writers' Guild Award for Best Original Radio Play.

Shelagh Stephenson was born in Northumberland and graduated with a drama degree from Manchester University. She has written five original plays for BBC Radio. These include *Darling Peidi*, about the Thompson and Bywaters murder case, which was broadcast in the Monday Play series in 1993; a Saturday Night Theatre, *The Anatomical Venus*, broadcast in the following year; and *Five Kinds of Silence* (1996), which won the Writers' Guild Award for Best Original Radio Play. Her first stage play, *The Memory of Water* opened at the Hampstead Theatre, London, in July 1996. She is currently working on new commissions for the Royal Exchange Theatre, Manchester and for the Hampstead Theatre, London.

Shelagh Stephenson

The Memory of Water
&
Five Kinds of Silence

Methuen Drama

Methuen Modern Plays

First published in 1997 by Methuen Drama

Copyright © 1997 by Shelagh Stephenson

Shelagh Stephenson has asserted her right
under the Copyright, Designs and Patents Act, 1988
to be identified as the author of this work

Published in the United Kingdom in 1997 by Methuen
Random House, 20 Vauxhall Bridge Road, London SW1V 2SA

Random House Australia (Pty) Limited
20 Alfred Street, Milsons Point, Sydney,
New South Wales 2061, Australia

Random House New Zealand Limited
18 Poland Road, Glenfield,
Auckland 10, New Zealand

Random House South Africa (Pty) Limited
Endulini, 5A Jubilee Road, Parktown 2193, South Africa

Distributed in the United States of America
by Heinemann, a division of Reed Elsevier Inc.
361 Hanover Street, Portsmouth, New Hampshire NH 03901 3959

Random House UK Limited Reg. No. 954009

A CIP catalogue record for this book is available from the British
Library

ISBN 0 413 71470 5

Typeset in 10.5 on 11.5pt Baskerville by
Wilmaset Ltd, Birkenhead, Wirral
Printed and bound in Great Britain by
Cox and Wyman Ltd, Reading, Berkshire

For Eoin O'Callaghan, with love

Contents

The Memory of Water

The Memory of Water was first performed at the Hampstead Theatre, London, on 11 July 1996, with the following cast:

Mary	Haydn Gwynne
Vi	Mary Jo Randle
Teresa	Jane Booker
Catherine	Matilda Ziegler
Mike	Alexander Hanson
Frank	Dermot Crowley

Directed by Terry Johnson
Designed by Sue Plummer
Lighting by Robert Bryan
Sound by John A. Leonard

Act One

Blackness. A pool of bluish green light reveals **Vi**, *aged around forty.
She is sitting at a dressing-table. The drawer is open. She wears a green
taffeta cocktail frock* circa 1962. *She is sexy, immaculately made-up,
her hair perfectly coiffed. She wears earrings and a matching necklace,
and carries a clutch bag, from which she takes a cigarette and lighter.
She lights up. The pool of light opens up to reveal the rest of the room in
a dim, golden, unreal glow: a bedroom, dominated by a double bed in
which* **Mary** *lies, wearing a pair of sunglasses. She watches* **Vi**. *The
room is slightly old-fashioned, with dressing-table and matching
wardrobe. Some clothes are draped over a chair. There is a long
diagonal crack running across the wall behind the bed. An open suitcase
lies on the floor, half unpacked, a half-full bottle of whiskey and a pile
of books on the bedside table.*

Mary   What do you want?

Vi   Someone's been going through these drawers.

Mary   Not me.

Vi   What did you think you'd find?

Mary   Nothing.

She closes the drawer and looks over to the bed.

Vi   That crack's getting worse. Have you noticed anything
about the view?

Mary   No.

Vi   It's closer.

Mary   What is?

Vi   The sea. Fifty yards closer. It'll take the house
eventually. All gone without a trace. Nothing left. And all
the life that happened here, drowned, sunk. As if it had never
been.

Mary   D'you remember a green tin box with
chrysanthemums on it?

Vi   No.

Mary   It had papers in it. It's gone. Where is it?

Vi   I've no idea.

Mary   What have you done with it?

Vi *picks up some books from the beside table and looks through the titles.*

Vi   'Head Injuries and Short Term Changes in Neural Behaviour' . . . 'The Phenomenology of Memory' . . . 'Peripheral Signalling of the Brain'.

She puts them down.

Bloody hell, Mary. What's wrong with Georgette Heyer?

Go to black. Fade up bedside lamp. **Vi** *has gone.* **Mary** *is lying prostrate. She stirs and gets out of bed, goes to the dressing-table, opens drawers, rifles through them. The phone rings.*

Mary   Hello? . . . What time is it? . . . I wouldn't be talking to you if I was, would I? I'd be unconscious . . . Where are you? . . . Jesus . . . you're what? So will you want me to pick you up from the station?

The door opens and **Teresa** *comes in.*

Teresa   Oh . . .

Mary   Hold on . . . (*To* **Teresa**.) It's not for you.

Teresa   Who is it?

Mary (*to caller*)   What? She's gone where? . . . OK, OK. I'll see you later. Are you sure you don't want me to pick you up –

She's cut off.

Hello? . . . Shit.

Teresa   Who was that?

Mary   A nuisance caller. We struck up a rapport.

Teresa   He's not staying here, is he?

Mary   Who?

Teresa I'm presuming it's your boyfriend.

Mary How much sleep have I had?

She picks up a portable alarm clock and peers at it.

Teresa How's his wife?

Mary Jesus. Two and a half hours.

She flops back on the pillows. Looks at **Teresa**.

Why are you looking so awake?

Teresa I've been up since quarter past five. Presumably he's leaving her at home, then.

Mary You've got that slight edge in your voice. Like a blunt saw.

Teresa I'm just asking –

Mary Of course he's bloody leaving her at home. She's gone to stay with her mother.

Teresa I thought she was ill.

Mary Maybe she went in an iron lung. Maybe she made a miracle recovery. I don't know. I didn't ask.

Teresa Where's he going to sleep?

Mary What?

Teresa You can't sleep with him in that bed.

Mary He's staying in an hotel.

Teresa I thought it might be something important.

Mary What?

Teresa The phone. Funeral directors or something.

Mary We've done all that. Can I go back to sleep?

Teresa And where's Catherine?

Mary She said she might stay over with someone.

Teresa Does she still have friends here?

Mary Probably. I don't know.

She turns away, settles down, and shuts her eyes. **Teresa** *watches her for a while.*

Teresa   She could have phoned to say. Anything could have happened to her. It's still snowing.

Mary   She's thirty-three, Teresa.

Teresa   The roads are terrible.

Mary   She'll get a taxi.

Teresa   Probably just as well she didn't come home. She'd have probably drunk four bottles of cider and been brought home in a police car. And then she'd have been sick all over the television.

Mary   She was thirteen when she did that.

Teresa   She was lucky she didn't get electrocuted.

Mary   It wasn't switched on.

Teresa   Yes it was, I was watching it. It was *The High Chaparral.*

Mary   No it wasn't. I wish you'd stop remembering things that didn't actually happen.

Teresa   I was there. You weren't.

Mary *gives up trying to sleep. Sits up.*

Mary   I was there.

Teresa   That was the other time. The time when she ate the cannabis.

Mary   That was me. I ate hash cookies.

Teresa   It was Catherine.

Mary   It was me.

Teresa   I was there.

Mary   So where was I?

Teresa   Doing your homework probably. Dissecting frogs. Skinning live rabbits. Strangling cats. The usual.

Mary Teresa. I'd like to get another hour's sleep. I'm not in the mood, OK?

She tries to settle down in the bed, and pulls something out that's causing her discomfort: a glass contraption with a rubber bulb at one end. She puts it on the bedside table and settles down again. Teresa picks it up.

Teresa Oh, for God's sake . . . Is this what I think it is?

Mary I don't know. What d'you think it is?

Teresa A breast pump.

Mary I found it on top of the wardrobe. I think I'd like to have it.

Teresa Why?

Mary Because you've got the watch and the engagement ring.

Teresa For Lucy. Not for me. For Lucy.

Mary OK. So you want the breast pump. Have it.

Teresa I don't want it.

Mary Good. That's settled. Now let me go to sleep.

Teresa You can't just take things willy-nilly.

Mary You did.

Teresa Oh, I see. I see what this is about.

Mary *sits up.*

Mary It's not about anything, it's about me trying to get some sleep. For Christ's sake Teresa, it's too early in the morning for this.

Mary *pulls the covers over her head. Silence.* **Teresa** *goes to the door, turns back.*

Teresa Could you keep off the phone, I'm waiting for Frank to ring and my mobile's recharging –

Mary If you take that phone to the funeral this time –

Teresa Oh, go to sleep.

Mary *sits up*.

Mary   I'm surprised Dad didn't burst out of his coffin and punch you.

Teresa   I didn't know it was in my bag.

Mary   You could have turned it off. You didn't have to speak to them.

Teresa   I didn't speak to them.

Mary   You did. I heard you. You told them you were in a meeting.

Teresa   You're imagining this. This is a completely false memory.

Mary   All memories are false.

Teresa   Mine aren't.

Mary   Yours in particular.

Teresa   Oh, I see, mine are all false but yours aren't.

Mary   That's not what I said.

Teresa   And what's with the Ray-Bans?

Mary *takes them off*.

Mary   I couldn't sleep with the light on.

Teresa   You could have turned it off.

Mary   I was frightened of the dark.

Teresa   When did this start?

Mary   It's all right for you. You're not sleeping in her bed.

Teresa   Oh, for goodness' sake.

Mary   You grabbed the spare room pretty sharpish.

Teresa   I was here first.

Mary   Have the sheets been changed?

Teresa   Yes.

Mary   When?

Teresa   What difference does it make?

Mary   I don't like sleeping in her bed, that's all.

Teresa   She didn't die in it.

Mary   She was the last person in it. It's full of bits of skin and hair that belong to her −

Teresa   Stop it −

Mary   And it makes me feel uncomfortable −

Teresa   What bits of skin and hair?

Mary   You shed cells. They fall off when you're asleep. I found a toenail before.

Teresa   Please.

Mary   I thought I might keep it in a locket round my neck. Or maybe you'd like it −

Teresa   Stop it, for goodness' sake.

Teresa *picks up a book from the bedside table.*

You can't leave work alone for five minutes, can you, even at a time like this?

Mary   I've a very sick patient.

Teresa   You had a very sick mother.

Mary   Don't start, Teresa.

Teresa   Oh, she never complained. Because your job's important. I mean, doctors are second to God, whereas Frank and I only have a business to run, so obviously we could drop everything at a moment's notice.

Mary   It's not my fault.

Silence.

Teresa   Why do we always do this?

Mary   What?

Teresa   Why do we always argue?

Mary   We don't argue, we bicker.

Teresa   OK, why do we bicker?

Mary   Because we don't get on.

Teresa   Yes we do.

Mary   Oh, have it your own way.

She unscrews the whiskey and takes a swig. **Teresa** *looks at her, aghast.*

Teresa   You haven't even got out of bed yet.

Mary   It's the only way we're going to get through this.

She offers it to **Teresa***, who shakes her head.*

Teresa   D'you often have a drink in the morning?

Mary   Of course I bloody don't, what d'you think I am?

Teresa   Lots of doctors are alcoholics. It's the stress.

Mary   Someone dies, you drink whiskey. It's normal, it's a sedative, it's what normal people do at abnormal times.

She takes another swig. Silence.

Mary   OK. Let's be nice to each other.

Silence.

What do people usually talk about when their mother's just died?

Teresa   I don't know. Funeral arrangements. What colour coffin. I've got a list somewhere.

Mary   There should be a set form. Like those books on wedding etiquette. Sudden Death Etiquette. Lesson One. Breaking the news. Phrases to avoid include: guess what?

Teresa   I was distraught, I wasn't thinking properly –

Mary   I thought you'd won the lottery or something –

Teresa   It's quite tricky for you, being nice, isn't it?

Mary   Sorry. I forgot. How are you feeling?

Teresa *looks at her watch.*

Teresa   I was expecting him to phone an hour ago.

Mary I'm not talking about Frank.

Teresa I don't know how I feel. Everything I eat tastes of salt.

Silence. **Teresa** *crosses the room and takes the whiskey from* **Mary**. *She takes a swig and grimaces.*

Teresa Salt. Everything tastes of it.

Hands it back. Sits on the bed.

Teresa The funeral director's got a plastic hand.

Mary God.

Pause.

Mary What's it like?

Teresa Pink.

Mary What happened to his real one?

Teresa How should I know?

Mary Didn't you ask him?

Teresa It didn't seem appropriate.

Mary No. I suppose not.

Teresa He was showing us pictures of coffins.

Mary As they do.

Catherine (*off*) Hi!

Mary Oh God.

Teresa In here.

Catherine *bursts in, wrapped in layers of coats and scarves, laden with carrier bags. She divests herself as she speaks.*

Catherine God, it's bloody freezing out there. It's like *Scott of the Antarctic*, the cab was sliding all over the place and I had one of those drivers who kept saying, have you been shopping, are you going somewhere nice? And I said, yes, actually, a funeral. My mother's. I thought, that'll shut him up, but it turns out he knew her. I forgot what it's like up here. Everyone knows the butcher's daughter's husband's mother's cat. And he got all upset, we had to pull over, so anyway I invited him to the funeral. He's called Dougie. I bet he doesn't come. God, I've got this really weird pain at the very bottom of my stomach, here, look, just above my pubic bone. It keeps going sort of stab, twist, so either I've got some sort of cyst, but actually, God, I know what it is, I bet. I bet I'm ovulating. Isn't that amazing? I can actually feel the egg being released. Although, hang on, I don't think I'm due to ovulate. You can't ovulate twice in the same month, can you? It's not my appendix because I haven't got one. Fuck. It must be PMT. In which case I think I've got an ovarian cyst.

Silence.

Mary   D'you want us to take you to hospital or shall I whip it out now on the kitchen table?

Catherine   I'll be fine.

Mary   Good, because I'm over the limit for either activity.

Catherine   Oh brilliant, whiskey.

She picks up the bottle and takes a slug.

Teresa   Where've you been?

Catherine   Shopping.

Teresa   Shopping?

Catherine   Well, you'd call it a displacement activity, but I call it shopping.

Teresa   All night?

Catherine   I went for a drink. I stayed with some friends.

Teresa   What friends?

Catherine   You don't know them. Oh God, there it goes again. Have you ever had this? Right here. Right at the bottom of your stomach?

Teresa   No.

Catherine   What d'you think it is?

Mary   I've no idea.

Teresa   We've been worried sick.

Catherine   Look, just here —

She takes **Mary**'*s hand and holds it against her groin.*

Mary   Wind.

Catherine   Do any of your patients actually survive?

Teresa   You could have picked up a phone. I mean, where've you been?

Catherine   Down the docks shagging sailors, what d'you think?

Mary   I'd have come with you if I'd known.

Teresa   It's just a bit insensitive —

Mary   Yes it is. There's a time and a place for everything —

Teresa   Disappearing, leaving us to deal with all this —

Catherine   All what? D'you like my shoes? I can't stop buying shoes. I even like the smell of them. Honestly, it's just like an eating disorder except it's not it's just shoes although sometimes it's underwear. D'you ever get that, you have to buy twenty pairs of knickers all at once, usually when you're a bit depressed —

Teresa   You can't wear those for a funeral. You look like Gary Glitter.

Catherine   I didn't buy them for the funeral.

Mary   I remember them the first time round. They were horrible then.

Catherine   I got them in a sale.

Mary   Oh well. That's some consolation.

Catherine   What's wrong with them?

Teresa   I thought you didn't have any money.

Catherine   Credit cards. What's wrong with them?

Teresa   You said you were broke.

Catherine   Oh, for God's sake, broke doesn't mean you can't buy things. I'm trying to cheer myself up, or is that not allowed? The minute I walk in the door I feel it in waves, the two of you waiting to pounce, looking for something to criticize. Christ, it's no wonder I've got low self-esteem.

Mary   You have an ego the size of Asia Minor.

Catherine   I'm just asking you to clarify your position *vis à vis* my shoes. I mean, quite obviously you don't like them, but why d'you always have to do this sneery superior thing? Why can't you just be straight and say you hate them?

Mary   I hate them. Can I go back to sleep now?

Teresa   I'm just wondering how you can afford to go out and buy all this stuff if you haven't got any money.

Mary   She shoplifts.

Catherine   Will someone tell me what I'm supposed to have done?

Mary   It was a joke.

Catherine   So all right, I know, Mum's dead –

Teresa   There's no need to put it like that –

Catherine   But you want me to sit down and cry about it and I can't.

Mary   I don't. I want you to go away.

Catherine   You always do this to me.

Mary   I'm tired.

Catherine   Some of the things you say to me are just, you know, not on. It's like I don't count. All my bloody life. And I'm not having it any more. I won't take it any more, OK?

Teresa   Have you been taking drugs, Catherine?

Catherine   Oh, for God's sake. I was in a really good mood till I walked in here.

Teresa   Your mother's just died, how can you be in a good mood? Try and be a bit more sensitive –

Catherine   No one's being sensitive to me.

Mary   We fucking are!

Silence.

Catherine   Did Xavier call?

Mary   Who?

Catherine   Xavier.

Mary   I thought he was called Pepe?

Catherine   You see, this is what you do to me. This permanent, constant, endless belittling.

Teresa   He didn't call.

Catherine   I'm about to marry him and you can't even get his name right.

Mary   You're always about to marry people.

Catherine   What's that supposed to mean?

Mary   And you never do.

Teresa   Oh shut up, both of you.

Silence.

Catherine   If I don't get some pain killers I'm going to die.

Mary   There might be some paracetamol in my case.

Catherine   Haven't you got anything more exotic?

Catherine *goes to the suitcase.*

Mary   Not for you, no. They're in the pocket. Now, will you both go away and let me get some sleep?

Teresa   Would anyone like some barley cup?

Catherine *finds the paracetamol and takes a couple.*

Catherine   I'd rather drink my own urine.

Mary   You may laugh.

Teresa   I do not drink my own urine.

Mary   Yet.

Catherine   Haven't we got any ordinary tea?

Teresa   That stuff in the kitchen's made from floor sweepings. You might as well drink liquid cancer.

Mary   God, you do talk absolute shite sometimes.

Teresa   Some people think that drinking your own urine –

Mary   Yes I know. And they're all mad.

Teresa   You're always so certain when it comes to things you know nothing about.

Mary   You know bugger all about bugger all.

Teresa   You've a completely closed mind, it infuriates me. You're so supercilious, you don't even listen –

Mary   If God had meant you to ingest your own urine, he'd have rigged up a drinking-straw arrangement directly from your bladder. To save you the indignity of squatting over a teacup. Now please, I just want an hour.

Teresa   There are things to do.

Mary   They can wait.

Catherine   I'm going to have a hot bath and a joint. I can't stand this.

She goes.

Teresa   So once again it's me. Everything falls to me.

Mary   Go and have a lie down, Teresa.

Teresa   I can't bloody lie down, I can't sit still. I can't cope, I need some Rescue Remedy.

She goes out.

Mary   I've got some beta blockers, they're much better –

Teresa (*off*)   I get agitated. I get like this. I don't need drugs.

She comes back, carrying her bag, chanting.

Teresa   Brown one-and-a-half pounds of shin of beef in a heavy casserole. Remove and set aside. Sauté two medium onions in the casserole with two crushed cloves of garlic –

Mary   What are you doing?

Teresa   Recipes. I recite recipes. It's very soothing. I've tried meditation but my mind wanders. I think of all the phone calls I should be making instead of sitting there going 'om'. Carbonnade of beef seems to work best.

Mary   You're a vegetarian.

Teresa   I've tried it with nut loaf but it's not the same. Add one finely chopped stick of celery, two carrots ditto and cook until soft and pale golden –

Mary   Normal people fantasize about sex. Not casseroles.

Teresa   And now I've got that salt taste in my mouth and I feel sick.

Mary   Psychosomatic.

Teresa   I know it's psychosomatic. I know it is, all right. I'd just like it to stop, that's all.

Catherine *comes in with a bundle of mail.*

Catherine   More fan mail.

Mary   I thought you'd gone for a bath to soothe your cyst.

Catherine   There's not enough water. So it's still sort of niggling, I wish it would stop –

She goes to her carrier bags and takes out various pieces of clothing. She opens the wardrobe door, holds them up against herself in front of the mirror.

I think it's stress. I mean it's an incredibly stressful time, isn't it, and I always get things like this when I'm strung out. Last year I had this weird thing in my legs, like they were kind of restless or jumpy or something. Every time I tried to go to sleep they used to sort of twitch and hop. The doctor in Spain said it was quite common and I just needed to relax more, but I can't, I've got an incredibly fast metabolism and then I get that spasm thing in my stomach which is definitely stress-related, I'm sure it's irritable bowel syndrome. I mean, that starts up the minute I'm even a tiny bit tense, I notice it straight away because I'm very in touch with my body, I can sort of hear it speaking to me.

Pause.

Teresa   I think I'm going mad.

Catherine   Last night I dreamed I could do yogic flying. I bet that means something –

She tugs at the jacket.

I'm not sure about this, are you? I don't suit black, that's the problem.

Teresa   As soon as the phone went I knew.

Catherine   Can you wear trousers at a funeral?

Teresa   I said to Frank, I can't answer it. We should never have left her at the hospital like that. We should have stayed.

Mary   You weren't to know.

Teresa   I'm not good with hospitals, I had to get away. Everyone in her ward looked like they'd already died, everyone was pale grey with a catheter.

Mary *is opening the mail. Reads.*

Mary   'With deepest sympathy on your sad loss, Mimi.' Who's Mimi?

Teresa   When Frank spoke to them they said, she's worse, you'd better get up to the hospital. I took the phone and said, she's dead isn't she, you don't phone at three in the morning unless someone's dead. And then, this is the awful bit, I put the phone down, and the thing I wanted to do more than anything else was have sex, which is sick, I know, that's what

Frank said afterwards. And then I ate a whole packet of rice
cakes and half a jar of marmalade in the car on the way to the
hospital. I don't even like marmalade. I know I should have
phoned you two, but I had this idea, this flicker she might not
be dead, even though I knew she was really, but they
wouldn't tell me over the phone, and I'd have woken you up,
and what would the point be anyway, you were miles away –

Mary   It's OK. Stop worrying about it –

Teresa   That's why I didn't phone straight away. Mimi
used to live three doors down.

Catherine   Can I borrow a skirt from someone?

Teresa   I keep going over and over it –

Catherine   Is anyone listening to me?

Mary   Oh, shut up and sit down. Your cyst might burst.

Teresa   And the doctor was about twelve, and
embarrassed. Eventually we had to say it for him. He kept
fiddling with his pen and giving us a run-down of everything
that had happened, until eventually Frank said, 'Are you
trying to tell us she's not coming back? Are you trying to tell
us she's dead?' And he said, 'More or less, yes.' And I said,
what d'you mean, more or less? She's either dead or she isn't,
you can't be a bit dead, for God's sake. And then I looked at
my feet and I was wearing odd shoes. A black one and a
brown one. Not even vaguely similar. So I started to laugh
and I couldn't stop. They had to give me a sedative. Frank
was shocked. They're not like us, his family, they've got
Italian blood. Someone dies, they cry. They don't get
confused and laugh.

Catherine   All I want to know is, can I borrow a skirt?

Mary   Oh shut up, Catherine, for Christ's sake!

Catherine   If I could get an answer out of anyone, I
would –

Mary   Yes, you can borrow a fucking skirt!

Silence. **Teresa** *goes to her bag and takes out a bottle of pills. She takes two.*

Catherine What are they?

Teresa Nerve tablets. Have one, for heaven's sake. Have six. Have the lot. They're completely organic, no chemicals.

Catherine I like chemicals.

Teresa (*emptying her bag on to the bed*) All right, don't then. I've got a list somewhere. Things to sort out.

Mary Do it later Teresa.

Teresa I can't. I can't sit still. I have to do it now.

Mary You're a useless advertisement for the health food industry.

Teresa Supplements. We do health supplements. Remedies. How many times do I have to tell you? You do this deliberately, you wilfully misinterpret what we do because you think it's funny or something, and actually I'm getting bored with it.

Catherine You're making me incredibly tense, both of you.

Teresa We're making you tense? Good God, you haven't stopped since you came in. Jumping around all over the place like you're on speed, which, thinking about it, you probably are, blahing on about your ovaries and your restless legs and your PMT. I don't give a toss about your insides. Has anyone seen my electronic organizer?

They look vaguely round the room. Silence.

Mary What does it look like?

Teresa I had it a minute ago, I had it –

Teresa *throws her bag down. Silence.* **Catherine** *offers her the joint.*

Catherine D'you want some of this?

Teresa No, thank you.

Mary Maybe you should.

Catherine It's completely organic. We grew it in the garden.

Teresa *takes a reluctant puff. Then another. Silence.*

Catherine You know when you went to the hospital. When she was dead . . .

Teresa Mmmm . . . ?

Catherine Did you see her?

Teresa Who?

Catherine Mum.

Teresa Of course I did.

Catherine How did she look?

Teresa Asleep. She just looked asleep.

Catherine *takes the joint back.*

Catherine Oh good.

Silence.

Teresa It's got the list on it. My organizer's got the list on it.

Mary We don't need a list.

Teresa I do.

Catherine Why?

Teresa Because I'm not functioning properly, d'you understand? I can't remember anything.

Catherine There's nothing to remember.

Teresa Funerals don't organize themselves, they don't just happen spontaneously.

Mary There's nothing left to organize. Stop panicking.

Teresa As soon as I heard the phone I knew.

Catherine *opens an envelope and reads a card.*

Catherine   'My thoughts are with you at this sad time. Your mother was a wonder woman. Norman Pearson.' Norman Pearson?

Teresa *takes the card from her and looks at it.*

Teresa   Patterson. Norman Patterson.

Mary   Who's he? And what does he mean 'wonder woman'?

Teresa   I don't know. He's got an allotment.

Catherine   We could organize the catering. We could do that. God, I'm starving. Is anyone else hungry?

Mary   Maybe they were having an affair.

Catherine   Munch munch munch, I'd really like some Shreddies. Have we got any Shreddies, d'you think?

Teresa   She was getting more and more confused. Everything was packing up. I tried everything. I offered her all sorts of things. I wanted to take her to that herbalist in Whitby. She wouldn't have any of it.

Mary   I don't think the colonic irrigation was a very good idea. Not for Alzheimer's Disease.

Teresa   You don't know the first thing about colonics –

Mary   I do know that your colon is specifically designed to function independently, without recourse to a foot pump.

Teresa   She never took care of herself, that's the problem.

Mary   She was seventy-five. She died. Let her be.

Teresa   She still smoked.

Mary   So what?

Teresa   She died because her heart gave out because she never ever looked after herself properly.

Mary   I don't think that's strictly true.

Teresa   You're a doctor, you know it's true.

Mary OK. It's all her own fault. She ate sliced white bread so she deserves to die. Whereas you wouldn't have it in the house, so you'll probably live to a hundred and twenty. You shove so many vitamins and antioxidants down your throat that you'll probably manage to avoid death altogether. That's the general idea, isn't it? While the rest of us deserve all we get, including lingering cancer, because we've been recklessly cavalier in the diet department. Or we couldn't quite stomach six feet of plastic tubing being shoved up our bottoms –

Teresa Thank God you're not my doctor –

Mary Thank God you're not my patient –

Teresa I'm just saying, if you eat properly –

Mary And I'm just saying people die. You can't avoid it. Not even you.

Teresa Well, you two managed to avoid it pretty comprehensively when it came to Mum. Most of the time you weren't even here.

Mary Great. The guilt fest. I knew we'd get there eventually.

Catherine It's no good trying to make me feel guilty because I don't.

Teresa I didn't think for a moment you would.

Catherine You'd like me to, though, and I won't. I refuse. I've nothing to feel guilty about at all. I didn't like her.

Mary Who?

Catherine Mum.

Teresa Don't be ridiculous.

Catherine She didn't like me.

Mary Yes she did.

Catherine How do you know?

Teresa She was your mother.

Catherine   I had a horrible childhood.

Teresa   We all had the same childhood. It wasn't horrible.

Catherine   Mine was.

Mary   That's because you're an egomaniac.

Catherine   She thought I was the menopause.

Mary   Who told you that?

Catherine   She did. She had the cat put down without telling me. She shut me in a cupboard. She said it was an accident but it wasn't.

Mary   When did she do all this?

Catherine   I never had the right shoes. She wouldn't let me visit you in hospital when you had an exploding appendix. She did it deliberately. She excluded me from everything. She made me stay in the shop after closing time and count nails.

Mary   When I think of our childhood, we went on a lot of bike rides and it was always sunny.

Teresa   Well, it was for you. You couldn't put a foot wrong.

Catherine   When I think of it, it was always pissing down. And what bike? I never had one.

Teresa   I'm sure you came to the beach with us, I remember it —

Catherine   The only time I went to the beach, it was with you and you left me there. You forgot me. You didn't remember till you got home and mum said, where's Catherine?

Teresa   That was Mary. She was too young, she was being a pain and showing off in Esperanto, so we ran away and left her. With no bus fare and the tide coming in.

Catherine   It was me!

Mary   No it wasn't. It was me.

Catherine   So how come I remember it?

Mary   Because I told you about it and you appropriated it because it fits. If it was horrible, it must have happened to you. And she didn't have the cat put down, it just died.

Teresa   It got run over by a combine harvester actually.

Catherine   I don't remember any of this.

Teresa   The amount of chemicals you've had through your system, I'm surprised you can remember anything at all.

Catherine   You did leave me at the beach. Someone left me at the beach. I remember it vividly. I've got a brilliant memory. I remember everything.

Teresa   You've forgotten Lucy's birthday every year since she was born —

Mary   You'd go mad if you remembered everything. What would be the point? Your head would burst. There's an illness actually, a sort of incontinent memory syndrome, where you recall everything, absolutely everything, in hideous detail, and it's not a blessing, it's an affliction. There's no light and shade, no difference between the trivial and the vital, no editing system whatsoever.

She looks at **Catherine**.

Actually, Catherine, maybe you should come in for a few tests.

Catherine   You're doing it again!

Teresa *has spied something under the bed. She picks it up: her electronic organizer.*

Teresa   I've found it. I've found my list.

She consults her gadget.

Insurance — undertakers 10.30, bridge rolls — I think there's just the flowers left —

Catherine   Do we have to do this now?

Teresa   It won't get done on its own. If it was up to you two, she'd have to cremate herself —

Mary   All right, all right —

Teresa   Because whilst you were doing Spanish dancing with Pepe in Fuengirola —

Catherine   His name's Xavier and I've never been to Fuengirola in my life —

Teresa   I was watching her fall apart. Twenty miles here, twenty miles back. Three times a week.

Catherine   I spoke to her a week ago. She wasn't that bad. She said she was off to the hairdressers.

Teresa   Oh, for goodness' sake, she was mad as a snake. And I'm the one who dealt with it all.

Mary   I'm sure when they publish a new edition of *Foxe's Book of Martyrs* they'll devote a chapter entirely to you.

Teresa   Every month something else went, another wire worked itself loose. Not big things, little things. She used to put her glasses in the oven. 'What day is it?' she'd say, and I'd say, 'Wednesday' and she'd say 'Why?' 'Well, it just is. Because yesterday was Tuesday.' And she'd say 'There was a woman here with a plastic bucket. Who is she?' 'Elaine. You know Elaine. Your home help.' And then she'd look at me and we'd start all over again. 'What day is it?' I mean, she wasn't even that old.

Silence. She takes some sheets of photographs from her bag.

Anyway. I got these photos from the florist. There's a number under each picture, so if you just give me the number of the wreath you want, I can phone in the order.

She hands the photos to **Mary***, who gives them a cursory glance.*

Mary   I'll have the one in the shape of a football.

Teresa   I'm just trying to keep things in a neutral gear, that's all.

Mary   Choosing flowers for your mother's funeral is not what I'd call a neutral activity.

The phone rings. **Teresa** *and* **Mary** *both make a grab for it.* **Mary** *wins.*

Mary   Hello? . . . Hello?

Catherine   Is it Xavier?

Mary   Hello?

Teresa   Give it to me.

Mary   There's just a crackling sound. Hello, can you hear me?

Teresa *grabs the receiver.*

Teresa   Frank?

Catherine   It'll be Xavier.

Mary *grabs it back.*

Mary   Mike?

The line goes dead. She puts the receiver down. Silence.

Mary   It's like waiting for the relief of Mafeking.

Silence.

Catherine   Does anyone want a sandwich?

Mary *gets out of bed and rifles through her suitcase for clothes.*
Catherine *begins to go.*

I went to this brilliant funeral in Madrid –

She goes out.

Mary   Brilliant. You went to a brilliant funeral.

Catherine (*off*)   He was a friend of Xavier's who fell off a roof and at the party afterwards they had little bowls of cocaine –

Mary   Oh, what a good idea. That'll go down well with the St Vincent de Paul Society.

Catherine (*off*)   And they dyed his poodle black. Just for the funeral. It was washable dye so it wasn't cruel, but anyway, it was raining and God, you should have seen the state of the carpets afterwards. So that was a bit of a disaster, but later on there was a firework display and he went up in a rocket.

Mary   Who?

Catherine (*off*)   The person who was dead. Not the poodle.

Mary   We're not doing that to Mum.

Catherine *reappears in the doorway carrying a bread knife.*

Catherine   I'm just saying that funerals don't have to be depressing. They can be quite happy.

Mary   Farcical even.

Catherine   Scrambled eggs. That's what I want. I bet we haven't got any eggs –

Exit **Catherine**.

Mary   I keep having dreams about her.

Teresa   Who?

Mary   Mum.

Teresa *opens a card.*

Teresa   Thank God. I thought you meant Catherine. It's bad enough having her in the same house without dreaming about her as well.

Mary   She's about fortyish and she's always wearing that green taffeta dress.

Teresa   'With deepest sympathy from Winnie and the boys. Sorry we won't be able to make the funeral due to a hip replacement op.'

Mary   I've never heard of any of these people, have you? And there's this smell in the dream.

Teresa   Can you dream smells?

Mary I think so.

Teresa I can't.

Mary It was that perfume she used to wear. In a tiny bottle, she got it in Woolworth's, and on Saturday night when she leaned over to say goodnight, she smelt of cigarettes and face powder and something alcoholic, and this perfume.

Teresa Phul Nana.

Mary Phul Nana . . . that was it . . . the whole room smelt of it.

Teresa She always said, if you don't wear perfume you'll never find a man.

Mary You'll never get a boyfriend.

Teresa And then, frankly –

Mary Unless you're a nun.

Teresa You might as well cut your throat with the bread knife.

Mary Slowly. A woman without a man is, well,

Teresa Hardly a woman at all.

Mary Might as well be a fish.

Teresa Of course, some women –

Mary Like your Auntie Betty –

Teresa Aren't bothered.

Mary Mind you, she was never much to look at.

Teresa Had a friend called Marjorie.

Mary But we won't go into that.

Teresa I blame the nuns.

Mary But anyway. Just you remember:

Both You don't want to end up like your Auntie Betty.

Mary I don't know how she managed to give birth to three daughters and then send us out into the world so badly equipped. She'd have sent us up K2 in slingbacks. With matching handbags.

Teresa   She must have taught us something, otherwise we'd all be dead.

Pause.

Did she ever mention sex to you?

Mary *gives her a withering look.*

Teresa   No, I suppose not.

Mary   I found a box of sanitary towels in her wardrobe once. I was nine. I said, what are these? I mean, I knew they were something bad, but I was desperate, I dared myself to ask. I was thinking all sorts of things. She snatched the box off me and said, 'Put that back. It's a home perm kit.'

There is a banging noise at the window.

Teresa   What was that?

Mary   There's something at the window . . .

Teresa   Hello . . . ?

The sound comes again.

Teresa   Oh God, it's like *Wuthering Heights*.

Mary   Someone wants to come in.

Teresa   Well, open the window.

Mary   You do it.

Teresa   Oh for goodness' sake –

She goes to the window and opens it, screams.

Mike   Sorry . . .

Mary   Mike . . . Oh Jesus . . . Teresa, this is Mike . . .

Teresa   Hello.

Mike   I've been ringing the doorbell.

Teresa   It's broken.

Mike   Yes.

Pause.

Mike   I'd like to come in, if that's not too much trouble.
Otherwise, you know, I could just stand here and die,
apparently it's a nice way to go, freezing, you don't feel a
thing, you just drift off into oblivion –

Mary   Oh God, yes, sorry, I'll open the door –

Mike   For Christ's sake –

He climbs in through the window, covered in snow.

Mary   How long have you been there?

Mike   Hours.

Mary   Sorry. Here, give me your coat.

Teresa   We thought you were Heathcliff. At the window.

Mike   Drink. I need a drink.

Mary (*taking off his outer clothes*)   Heathcliff wasn't at the
window. He was inside. It was Cathy trying to get in.

Mike   Sorry?

Teresa   Are you sure?

Catherine *appears, eating a sandwich and smoking another joint.
She has a glass in her hand.*

Catherine   Who's this?

Mary   Mike, this is Catherine. Catherine, this is Mike.

He tries to smile.

Mike   Sorry, can't speak. Frozen.

Catherine   Mike the married boyfriend Mike?

Mary *fetches the whiskey.*

Teresa   Would you like a cup of tea?

Catherine   You don't look a bit like you do on the
television. You're quite small really, aren't you?

Mike   People say this to me all the time, but I'm not
actually.

Catherine Mind you, you'd never think Robert Redford was only five foot five, would you?

Mary *snatches the glass from* **Catherine**.

Mary Give me that.

Fills it and gives it to **Mike**.

Catherine They always do this to me. So, how tall are you?

Mike I'm five eleven.

Catherine Don't be ridiculous, I don't believe you.

Teresa *hisses at her.*

Teresa Catherine . . .

Catherine Sorry, would you like some drugs?

She holds the joint out to him. **Mike** *shakes his head.*

Are you not allowed?

Mary He doesn't. Come here, sit down.

He sits on the bed and she rubs his hands, undoes his shoes and takes them off.

Mike I think I've got frostbite.

Catherine I won't tell anyone. Or I'll say you did but you didn't inhale.

Mike I'm sorry?

Catherine That's what celebrities usually say.

Mary He's not a celebrity, he's a doctor.

Catherine I saw your programme yesterday. That woman with the psoriasis. God. I thought you were really good.

Mike Thank you –

Catherine But you don't want to be caught with a joint in your hand, do you? On top of everything else. You can't be a drug addict *and* be having an affair. Can you imagine the

papers? 'TV Doctor blew my mind says hospital
consultant' –

Mary   Catherine you're off your face –

Teresa   Why don't you come with me and make some tea
for everyone?

Catherine   Our mother's just died.

Mike   I know. I'm very sorry.

Catherine *bursts into tears.*

Mary   I'm sorry about this, Mike. Catherine, stop it –

Catherine   God, is no one allowed to show their feelings
around here? I'm depressed, I've suffered a bereavement, it's
normal to cry, for God's sake –

Mary   Go away, stop doing this –

Mike   It's OK, it's OK, she's allowed to be unhappy –

Catherine   You see? It's only you two who are weird, you
don't know what it's like –

Teresa (*storming out*)   That's it. I'm getting a gun.

Catherine *throws herself on the bed and howls.*

Catherine   We're orphans . . .

Mike *puts his arm around her. She holds on to him, puts her head in his
lap.*

Catherine   And I'm the youngest, I had them for less time
than everyone else did . . .

Mary   Catherine, get up off that bed and get out –

Mike   She's OK, she can't help it, what's the matter with
you?

Mary   And you shut up, you know nothing. Catherine, if
you don't get out of here, so help me God, I'll brain you.

Catherine *gets up weakly, weeping. She manages to look tiny and
pathetic. She turns as she gets to the door.*

Catherine   I've got that pain again . . .

Mike   What pain? Where?

She totters over to **Mike** *and lifts her sweater up.*

Catherine   Just here . . .

Mary   There's nothing wrong with you.

Catherine   She keeps saying that to me −

The phone rings. She stops weeping immediately, and grabs it.

Hello? . . . Xavier? . . . Fuck . . . OK . . . OK . . . You're where? OK, I'll tell her.

She slams the phone down.

It's bloody Frank . . .

She storms out and slams the door.

Catherine (*off*)   Teresa!

Mary   I'm sorry. I'm sorry. You have to just ignore her. You don't understand.

Mike   Why are you being so horrible to her?

Mary   Where d'you want me to start?

Mike   OK, OK, OK, come here −

She puts her arms around him and they kiss. It grows passionate. Eventually she pulls away.

Mary   This is my mother's bed.

Mike   I know. Sorry. So.

Mary   So.

Mike   How are you?

Mary   Fine.

Mike   Good.

Mary   Is something wrong?

Mike   I've been stuck on a train in a snowdrift all night.

Mary   Sorry.

Pause.

Did you bring that paper I asked you for?

Mike *squirms apologetically*.

Mike I couldn't remember the title.

Mary 'A Trophic Theory of Neural Connections.' Why didn't you write it down?

Mike I didn't think, I mean, I didn't realize you needed it that badly. I thought you'd have enough on your plate. I mean, it's ridiculous, it's an obsession. What's the big deal about this patient? You've seen post-traumatic amnesia before, it's not that unusual —

Mary It's not an obsession. I've got close to him, that's all.

Mike How can you get close to someone who can't remember his own name?

Mary Forget it. I'll look up the paper when I get back.

Pause.

Everything all right at home?

Mike The same, you know.

Pause.

Mary Mike.

Mike What?

Mary D'you love me?

Mike Yes.

Mary Say it then.

Mike I love you. Now you.

Mary Now I what?

Mike Now you say it. That's the form.

Mary Oh, this is ridiculous.

Mike You started it.

Silence.

Mary So. She's better then?

Mike   Who?

Mary   Chrissie.

Mike   No. Why? What d'you mean?

Mary   I saw a photo of the two of you. In the hospital magazine. At a tombola, for Christ's sake. And there she was, large as life. Fit as a fiddle. And I thought, where's the intravenous drip? What happened to her catheter? I suppose it spoilt the line of her dress, did it?

Mike   Mary –

Mary   I'm sorry, I can't help it, it brings out something horrible in me. I mean you always give the impression she's at death's door, practically in an iron lung –

Mike   Don't exaggerate –

Mary   I'm exaggerating? You said she could hardly walk. Well, forgive me, but either that picture's trick photography, or she's doing the shagging twist –

Mike   She was feeling a bit better.

Mary   God, what's the matter with me? It's Catherine, she makes me want to kill people, and right now I want to kill your wife, which is irrational and I'm sorry.

Mike   You're in shock.

Mary   I'm not in shock. But let me just say this: people don't get off their deathbeds for a tombola.

Mike   I'm sorry I went to a party with my wife. I'm sorry she's not as ill as you'd like her to be. Perhaps you'd prefer her to be dead too. For fuck's sake, Mary. What d'you want me to say?

Mary   I feel humiliated! I've rationalized, I've philosophized, I've come to terms with the fact that I'm living in some nether world with different rules where we don't do Christmas, we don't do bank holidays, and if you die I'll be the last to find out. I accept this because your wife's supposed to be incapable of crossing the street on her own, and now I discover her hopping round a dance floor like a bag of ferrets. I know I'm not supposed to feel things like humiliation or fury or jealousy because they're irrational but sometimes I do, sometimes I just do, OK?

Silence.

Mike I'm sorry.

Pause.

I think I've got hypothermia. Can I get into bed? I'll keep my clothes on.

Mary She'd probably quite like the idea of a man in her bed. Get in.

He gets into bed. She sits down on the chair.

Mike Don't stay over there. Come and sit with me.

Mary I'm fine here.

Mike Come on. Please. I've come all this way. The heating broke down on the train, the lights went, and just when we thought we were out of the woods, there were frozen points, and the buffet car ran out of food. We sat in the middle of nowhere and I started to worry about who we'd eat first if things got really out of hand. The man opposite me looked like Margaret Rutherford. I tried to imagine filleting him with a pocket penknife.

Mary I'll sit on the bed. I'm not getting into it.

She perches primly next to him. He kisses her. She brings her feet up, but pulls her mouth away from his. Lies next to him on top of the covers. He puts his arm round her.

Mary I'm sorry. This is making me very tense. It just feels weird.

Mike Sorry, sorry, sorry.

He puts his hands behind his head.

Mary He can remember his own name actually.

Mike Who?

Mary   That patient. It's coming back in bits. If you show him a bike, he can ride it. He can't remember what it's called, that's all.

Mike   I was talking to someone the other day who'd worked in this lab in France a few years back . . . or maybe he knew someone who worked there, I can't remember. Anyway, they were doing these experiments with water, because they were researching the efficacy of homeopathy, and what they came up with after months and months of apparently stringent tests was that you can remove every last trace of the curative element from a water solution and it will still retain its beneficial effect. And they decided that this meant water was like magnetic tape. That water had memory. You can dilute and dilute and dilute, but the pertinent thing remains. It's unseen, undetectable, untraceable, but it still exerts influence. I mean they did a full range of tests. It wasn't just a shot in the dark.

Pause.

It's all complete bollocks, of course. Except . . .

Mary   Except what?

Mike   I've got an erection.

Pause.

Mary   We can't. We absolutely can't.

Mike   No.

Mary   It'll go away if we ignore it.

He leans over and kisses her. After a while she pulls away and gets up. She walks about the room, picking up objects from the dressing-table, putting them down.

Mary   Everything I look at makes me want to cry. I see these things and a life unravels in front of my eyes. I can't sleep for remembering.

Mike   What?

Pause. **Mary** *is nervous.*

Mary Can you feel nostalgia for something that never really existed? I remember growing up here. I remember nightlights and a doll's house. I can see them in my mind's eye. And I'm not sure we had either. I find myself aching, longing for it. This half-imagined childhood.

Mike You want to be a child again?

Pause.

Mary I want to go through it again. The light on the landing, the bedtime stories. Even though I know some of the memories aren't real. It's like I've hooked up to some bigger, general picture, and it *feels* so real I can taste it.

Pause.

I think I'm pregnant.

Pause.

Mike What?

Mary You heard me.

Mike You can't be.

Mary I am.

Mike You can't possibly be.

Mary I know I'm geriatric, but I'm not completely dessicated —

Mike Hang on a minute, this is ridiculous —

Mary It's not ridiculous.

Mike Have you done a test?

Mary No, but I feel very strange.

Mike What d'you mean, strange?

Mary As in I'm-pregnant strange, what d'you think I mean?

Mike I'm a bit shocked, what did you expect? It's a bit of a fucking shock . . .

Mary   I'm telling you I'm pregnant, I'm not telling you I've got terminal cancer –

Mike   I'm not going to believe this till you've done a test.

Mary   I'm the size of a house. Look at me.

Mike   You always look like that, don't you?

Mary   Observant. There's another thing you're not.

Pause.

I feel weird.

Mike   You can't. You can't feel weird.

Mary   Well, I do.

Mike   This is unreal. This is completely unreal. I don't believe this is happening –

Mary   Stop getting in a state, will you?

Mike   I'm not getting in a fucking state!

Silence.

What are you going to do?

Mary   What am *I* going to do? What happened to *we*?

Mike   OK, OK, we.

Mary   Well I kind of hoped for the usual. You know, nine months' gestation followed by birth of something small and squalling. Preferably human. Or perhaps I'm asking for too much.

Mike   Let's not panic about it, OK?

Mary   I'm not panicking. You are.

Mike   I'm not. I'm not. I mean you're probably not. Pregnant.

Mary   I am.

She climbs on the bed next to him and kisses him. Puts her hand on his groin.

Brilliant. I'm pregnant. Instant detumescence.

Silence.

Mike I think . . . I don't think . . . you know, I mean, the thing is, I'm trying to say −

Mary It might make the papers, your wife will be humiliated, you can't cope and you're leaving me.

Mike No, that's not what I'm trying to say.

Pause.

You're sure you're pregnant?

Mary Would you like it in writing?

Mike I have to tell you there's a problem here. The thing is. How can I put this? The thing is, it's not mine. I mean if you are, it's not mine −

Mary Just run that past me again, will you?

Mike I've had a vasectomy.

Silence.

Mary What?

Mike I've had a vasectomy.

Mary You've had a vasectomy.

Mike Yes.

Silence.

Mary When?

Mike Before I met you.

She stares at him.

I wanted to tell you. I was going to, and then . . . it didn't seem important I suppose . . .

Mary It didn't seem important.

Mike No . . . I mean . . . I just . . . You never . . . I mean it never came up . . . I thought you didn't want children. You never said. I thought, you know, you had a career and everything.

Mary   You've got a career. You've also got three children.

Mike   I'm sorry. I'm sorry. Why didn't you say anything? Why didn't you tell me you wanted a child?

Mary   I'm thirty-nine, Mike. I'm thirty-nine. Didn't you ever think?

Mike   I'm not a mind-reader. You never showed the slightest sign. You never even hinted.

Pause.

Mary   I thought you'd leave me.

Mike   You thought I'd leave you?

Mary   I thought you'd leave me if I said I wanted a child.

The door opens and **Teresa** *comes in carrying a lot of black bin liners.*

Teresa   You're going to hate me for this – oh, for goodness' sake.

Mary *and* **Mike** *spring apart.* **Mary** *gets up.*

Mary   We were just talking.

Mike *gets out of bed.*

Mike   Look, fully dressed –

Catherine *comes in with another joint.*

Catherine   Oh God, have you two been in bed? That's disgusting.

Mary   What? Look, Mike and I are trying to have a conversation –

Teresa   We have to sort out her clothes.

Catherine   Why do we have to do it now?

Teresa *is already taking clothes out of the wardrobe.*

Teresa   A friend of mine's sending a truck to Zimbabwe and I promised I'd have then ready this afternoon.

Mary She's not even in her grave yet, and apart from
that —

Teresa If we wait until after the funeral, I'll get left with it
all. You two have to get back and Frank and I'll end up
doing it. And I think we should all do it.

Mary Teresa, listen —

Teresa No. You listen. If it wasn't for me, nothing would
ever get done. She'd be lying on the floor stoned out of her
brains, you'd be having it off in our dead mother's bed and
I'd be holding the fort —

Catherine St Teresa of Avila —

Teresa Somebody has to be practical! Somebody has to be
in charge, you two can live in chaos but I can't —

Catherine What chaos?

She is rifling through the clothing, holding frocks up in front of herself.

What's this made of, d'you think? Is it silk?

Mike Maybe I should, you know —

Mary Don't even think about it —

Mike Fine.

Mary I'm in shock, I still can't believe you —

Teresa The sooner we get this over with the better. Right.
I've worked it out. We divide it into two lots. Crap and good
stuff.

Catherine The crap we send to the poor bastards in
Zimbabwe —

Teresa The crap we take to the dump.

Catherine I quite like this. Can I have it?

She holds up a dress in front of her and hands the joint to **Teresa**, *who
puffs at it absent-mindedly as she sorts through the clothes.*

Mike Um, what would you like me to do?

Mary I don't know. Hang yourself.

She picks up the whiskey and takes a slug.

Mike   D'you think you should be drinking? I mean –

Mary   Just lie down and die, will you?

Teresa   Mike, you take these bags. This one for rubbish, this one for good stuff. We'll hand it to you, you pack it.

Mike   Right. OK. This one rubbish, this one good stuff . . .

Teresa *takes another armful from the wardrobe and throws it on the bed.* **Mary** *stands stricken, staring at it.* **Catherine** *is posing in mirrors, holding up frocks.*

Teresa   Oh for goodness' sake, Mary. I know it's not a very nice job, but it has to be done.

Mary   OK, OK.

She picks up some clothes dispiritedly. **Catherine** *picks up a gaudy floral number.*

Catherine   God, d'you remember this? What a mistake.

She dances round with the dress in front of her.

Teresa   I think that can go in the crap pile.

Catherine   They might like it in Zimbabwe.

Teresa   She wore that terrible hat with it, d'you remember?

Catherine *scrabbles through the pile. She picks up a hat.*

Catherine   Here it is, here it is –

Teresa *begins to giggle. She takes another puff of the joint.*

Mary   Is this what you add up to? A wardrobe full of tat and three pelican children?

Teresa   Oh dear, I do feel lightheaded . . . have some of this, Mary, it's all so much easier . . . pure thingy . . .

Catherine   Grass.

Teresa   Exactly, no chemicals.

She takes one more draw and hands the joint to **Mary**. **Catherine** *has put the hat on, and is draping the dress around her.*

Teresa   Cousin June's wedding. 1969.

Catherine   It was horrible even then. D'you remember we didn't want to sit next to her in church.

Mary   Give it to me. (*Takes it, hands it to* **Mike**.) This is for the rubbish.

Mike   Are you sure? Maybe we should have another bag for kind of in-betweens.

Catherine *snatches the dress back.*

Catherine   No, no it's you, Mary, it's perfect –

She holds it against **Mary** *who throws it aside.* **Mike** *puts it in the rubbish.* **Teresa** *yells.*

Teresa   Aargh, look at this –

She pulls out a sixties cocktail frock from the pile on the bed. **Catherine** *doubles up with laughter.*

She can't have worn this, surely.

Catherine   She did, I remember it, oh God, give it here.

She takes the dress and begins to struggle out of her clothes.

Mary   Catherine, for Christ's sake –

Catherine   I'm wearing underwear. Anyway, he's a doctor, stop being such a pain –

There is a great cry of triumph from **Teresa**, *who has been rooting around in the pile.*

Teresa   Yes!

She brings out a wild pink dress, circa 1963.

This was her Alma Cogan phase. Which I think, on reflection, I prefer to the crimplene phase that followed it.

Mary   Teresa, are we sorting out these clothes or not because I've got better things to do at the moment?

Teresa I mean what *was* crimplene, was it a sort of by product of formica?

She is holding the dress up against her in front of the mirror.

Mary Oh, this is ridiculous –

Teresa Actually, margarine, you know, is a by product of plastic. Or is it petrol?

Catherine *has got the dress on, and a hat.*

Catherine What d'you think? Is it me?

Teresa *laughs with stoned hysteria. Even* **Mike** *laughs.*

Mary And I don't know why you're laughing –

The room is in chaos. **Catherine** *and* **Teresa** *are unstoppable now.* **Catherine** *is trying on shoes, hats, lipstick. Earrings, anything.*

Teresa Turn away, Mike, turn away –

She goes behind the wardrobe door.

Mary I give up. Give that to me.

She takes the rubbish sack from **Mike** *and starts to stuff clothing into it.*

Mary Who did it?

Mike What?

Mary The operation. Who did the operation?

Mike Charlie Morgan. Why?

She starts to laugh.

Mary Charlie Morgan?

Catherine Who's Charlie Morgan? Oh, look, I've found a hairpiece from before the Boer War. Look at this –

Mike Is there a problem with that?

Mary No, no, no. Honestly.

Teresa *emerges from behind the wardrobe door, looks in the mirror.*

Teresa Oh God, what do I look like?

Mike   So what's funny?

Mary   Charlie-whoops-I've-made-a-bit-of-a-hash-of-this-Morgan.

Mike   Oh, for God's sake, that's a slanderous rumour, he's OK.

Mary   He's in a clinic at the moment. Drying out.

Mike   He did me years ago. He was steady as a rock.

Mary   You didn't notice an overpowering smell of aftershave?

Mike   Christ. He wasn't drinking it, was he?

Teresa (*scrabbling around in the bottom of the wardrobe*) Where're those pink shoes?

Mary   He's about to be struck off –

Catherine   Oh, look at this –

Mary   Gross professional negligence, I think it was –

Catherine   Mary, this is you –

She holds out the green dress which **Vi** *wore at the beginning of Act One.*

Teresa   Oh, put it on –

Mike   Are you sure?

Mary   Give me some of that joint, Catherine – positive –

Teresa   D'you think I need a handbag with this?

Mary   I can't believe you went to Charlie Morgan. Did he give you a special price or something?

Mary *takes the dress and starts to struggle into it, giggling.*

Mike   Are you making this up?

Catherine   Go for it, Mary!

Mary   Performing microsurgery when he was so drunk he had double vision.

Mike   I think you're exaggerating a bit –

Mary   I am not –

Catherine   You need bigger hair. Big, crispy hair.

Teresa   Yes, you see, you didn't get shiny hair in those days, did you? Honestly, all that hairspray, think of the carcinogens. Now, d'you think this bag or this –

She holds up two. **Mary** *has got the frock on now.*

Mary   There. What d'you think?

Catherine   You look dead like mum.

Momentary silence, before they realize, then screeches of appalled laughter. **Teresa** *and* **Catherine** *roll on the bed, clutch their sides. Wild, stoned hysteria, etc.* **Mary** *joins in. The door opens and* **Frank** *comes in, in his overcoat, carrying a suitcase.*

Frank   What the fuck . . . ?

Silence.

Teresa   Frank . . .

Frank   What are you doing?

Mary   We're sorting out mum's clothes . . .

Pause.

Catherine   D'you think we're sick?

Frank *looks at his watch.*

Frank   It's taken me fourteen hours to get here from Dusseldorf. I spent six of those sitting next to a woman from Carlisle who runs a puppet theatre for the deaf. She'd maroon hair and drank an entire bottle of gin whilst telling me about her alcoholic father who once bit the head off a chicken. She was wearing a dress that looked like a candlewick bedspread and she'd been on a course in Cologne learning mime and North African devil dancing. I thought, take me back to sanity. And I walk in on this. Pan's bloody People.

Silence. The women suppress their hysteria.

Mike   I'm Mike. Hi.

Frank   How d'you do. And then I got diverted to East Midlands.

Mike   Goodness.

Frank   What is it with this country? It's too hot, it's too cold, there's leaves on the line, it's the wrong sort of snow –

Catherine   Frank, chill out, have some drugs –

They all begin to giggle uncontrollably.

Frank   How long have they been like this?

Mike   I think it's the grief, you know . . .

The women get more hysterical. They hold on to each other and look at themselves in the mirror. They scream with laughter.

Mary   Oh God, what do we look like.

Catherine   Where's my camera, where's my camera?

She goes to her bag and scrabbles around. Pulls out camera.

Teresa   Oh yes, we've got to have a photo –

Frank   Don't be ridiculous –

Catherine   Frank, you take it –

She hands it to him. They all chant together like a football mob.

All   Photo, photo, photo –

Frank   OK, OK . . .

The women chant and pose and laugh hysterically.

Christ, they're a handful when they all get together. They just gang up, you'll get used to it . . . all right, all right, pull yourselves together . . . Where d'you want to be . . . ?

They all line up in front of the bed, linking arms and staggering and pushing each other.

Mary   OK, OK, smile everyone!

Catherine   I want to be in the middle!

They arrange and re-arrange themselves. **Frank** *takes a photo. A flash. Freeze frame: the women smiling in a row, arms linked. We* *realize there's a fourth person in the line-up:* **Vi***, smiling, cigarette held aloft, in her green taffeta dress. There's a white streak in her hair.* **Mary** *wheels round on her as* **Frank** *takes another photo. Freeze-frame the line-up, but with* **Mary** *caught looking at her mother, stricken. Slow lights change, music.* **Vi** *goes to sit at the dressing-table.* **Catherine** *and* **Teresa** *are still laughing.*

Teresa   Have you ever seen me more alluring? I'm a sex goddess, you have to admit it, Frank –

The phone rings. Lights change. The mood is still slightly hysterical. As **Teresa** *picks up the phone.*

Teresa   Hello? . . . Yes . . . What? . . . The what? . . .

The mood begins to sober as they listen.

Oh, I see . . . Yes . . . of course. Where are you? I'll get someone to – yes . . . OK . . .

She puts the phone down.

Social services want the zimmer frame back. They're on their way.

Frank   You'd better get out of the Widow Twanky get-up, or they'll have you all sectioned.

There's an awkwardness now. They feel sheepish, uncomfortable in their ridiculous outfits.

Teresa   And their van's stuck in a snow drift at the bottom of the road, they want someone to give them a push.

She looks at **Mike** *and* **Frank***.*

Mike   Of course, yes, right, OK, no problem, absolutely.

He pulls on his coat and boots.

Frank   Great. Just what I feel like. Some serious exertion in sub-zero temperatures. Who needs sleep?

Teresa *is gathering up her clothes.*

Teresa   I'll get the frame for you.

They go out. **Catherine** *and* **Mary** *are left.* **Mary** *looks white.*

Mary   Go and have your bath, Catherine.

Catherine *looks at the mess.*

Catherine   Who's going to sort all this out?

Mary   I'll do it.

Catherine *picks up her clothes and goes out.* **Vi** *and* **Mary** *look at each other.*

Vi   You look ridiculous in that.

Mary   The tin with the chrysanthemums on it. The one you don't remember. Where is it?

Vi   I told you. I've no idea.

Mary   What have you done with it?

Pause.

Where is it, Mum?

Go to black.

Act Two

Scene One

Vi and **Mary** are where they were when we left them. **Mary** is beginning to struggle out of her dress and back into her normal clothes. **Vi** gives her a long look.

Vi You need a bit of colour on your face. You were always pasty.

Mary Don't change the subject. Where's the tin?

Pause.

Vi Have you tried the shed?

Mary No.

Vi It might be in the shed.

Mary I'll look then.

Vi Although it might not. It's been years since I saw that tin. It had toffees in it originally. From Torquay. I'd have liked to have gone there. They have palm trees. I've never seen a palm tree in real life. I expect you've seen dozens. You're probably sick to death of palm trees.

Mary pulls on jeans and sweaters.

I do wish you'd wear something a bit more feminine occasionally.

Mary Apparently I look ridiculous. I'm going to look for the tin.

She begins to go but **Vi** stops her.

Vi This patient. The one you've got all the books about. What's wrong with him?

Mary He got hit on the head and lost his memory.

Vi gives a soft laugh.

Vi So what's your prognosis? Doctor.

Mary He'll recover. More or less intact. I think.

Vi Intact. I like that word. Intact. Everything in order. In the bag. Right as ninepence. That's nice. Was he in a fight?

Mary No, he opened a cupboard and a jar fell on him.

Vi Must have been a big jar.

Mary Pickled bell peppers.

Vi You wouldn't get pickled bell peppers up here. Probably a good thing. They sound dangerous.

Mary Can I go now?

Vi *has taken a dress from the pile.*

Vi Look. D'you remember this?

Mary No.

Vi I loved this dress. It was the only dress your father ever bought me.

She begins to dance. It's slightly seductive and sensuous.

Saturday nights I used to wear this. The men loved me, you know. Oh yes. All the men loved me. And I loved the men. I never cared for the women. I never liked them. Once I got my first bra I couldn't be doing with them any more.

Mary Pity you had three daughters really, isn't it?

Vi stops dancing.

Vi You put words into my mouth. Every one of you does it, but you in particular, you mangle everything into something else. My comedy mother. My stupid, bigoted, ignorant mother.

Mary Well you shouldn't say such stupid things.

Vi You lie in bed with your lovers and you tell stories about me. None of them complimentary. Most of them complaining. None of them true.

Mary Excuse me. I'm going to look for that tin.

She turns to go.

Vi   Don't walk away from me! You've done that all your life.

Mary *turns round, like a guilty child.* **Vi** *picks up a book from the bedside table and opens it at random.*

(*Reading.*) 'A biological memory system differs from a simple information storage device, by virtue of its inherent ability to use information in the service of its own survival . . . A library, for example, couldn't care less about its own survival. The problem is not one of storage. The problem is the difference between a dead and a living system.'

She shuts it.

So there's a difference between a cat and a bookcase. I could have told him that.

She looks at the price on the back of the book.

Twenty-five ninety-nine. My God.

Puts it down.

I don't know how this happened. I look at you and I think, you've come out wrong, all of you. There's something not quite right about how you've turned out. Not what I expected.

Mary   What a pity. After all your sterling efforts.

Vi   You seem like nice, personable people. I expect you are, but I don't know what you've got to do with me. You're closed off. I can't seem to get the hang of any of you. You don't tell me anything. I tell you things. What I did, where I went. And you just look irritated. You've no patience with me. No tolerance. And I had years of patience with you. It's not fair. How dare you? That's what I feel. How dare you?

Mary   How dare I what?

Vi   Sometimes when I'm talking and I know you're not really listening, I could tear your heads from your bodies. I could tear you apart with my teeth. All of you. You behave as if I'd no hand in the making of you. I took you on picnics, I got up in the night for you. And you remember the things you didn't have. Holidays not gone on. Bicycles never got. A particular type of shoe. How was I to know? When are we going to be done with this? I hear you talking and I think your memories aren't the same as mine. I remember the time of your childhood, and it seems to me that you don't remember it because you weren't there –

Mary   Why are you doing this to me? Why don't you do it to Teresa or Catherine?

Vi   How d'you know I don't?

She strokes the clothes left on the bed.

All my lovely dresses.

Mary   I'm sorry. It's not as if you're going to be needing them.

She begins to stuff them into black bags.

Vi   You were in my bed with him.

Mary   He was cold. We didn't do anything.

Vi   You wanted to.

Mary   Has nothing changed? You used to read my diaries, you knew about every boyfriend I ever had. You used to poke about my room. I always knew you were doing it, I used to watch you.

Vi   I had good reason.

Mary   You did not. D'you understand? You did not. Ever. Nothing gave you the right to sift through my life like that.

Vi   What is it you don't have? What's the word? Humility, is that it? I've watched you being offered the world on a plate. And all of it you've taken, without a backwards glance. Lovers, sex. Exotic sex probably. Whatever that is. All tasted and discarded. You take it in your stride, these trips to Paris, these shoes from Milan, this bottle of wine and not that one, this man and not that one. This choosing and refusing –

Mary You know nothing –

Vi I know different things. I know wanting and no choice. That counts too. It's not nothing. A shop, your father said, and I saw dresses and pink bath salts. What I got was bags of nails and grouting cement. Excitement was a delivery of ornamental door-knockers. You drink champagne because you feel like it, you buy things with plastic cards. I've wanted that. I've tasted bile in my mouth with wanting it. And you carry it so lightly, you're not even grateful. I look at your easiness with the world and I don't know how I spawned you. But I started it. I taught you to speak properly, I saved you from your own stupid mistakes –

Mary It wasn't stupidity, it was ignorance, and for that I blame you –

Vi I made sure you'd get somewhere, I made sure of it –

Mary Your idea of getting somewhere was marrying a dentist in a sheepskin coat from the Rotary Club –

Vi You invent these versions of me and I don't recognize myself –

Mary I'm not listening to you –

Vi You never did –

Mary I listened. I did what you wanted. It was you who didn't listen to me.

Vi I hear your stories. None of it's true. You invent it. You invent me. I'm proud of you and you're ashamed of me –

Mary I am not –

Vi I hear you say it all the time. I'm not like my mother, I'm not, I'm not. I'm like my father. Look in the mirror. Why can't you see it? Everyone else can. Look at the curve of your cheek, look at your hands, the way they move. You're doing it now. That's me. I got it from my mother. She got it from her mother. And on it goes, so far back that we don't know who began it or on what impulse, but we do it, we can't help it –

Mary   I've inherited some of your gestures. So what?

Vi   Don't try and reinvent yourself with me. I know who you are.

Mary   You don't know anything.

Vi   I look at you and I see myself.

Mary   Have you finished?

Vi   Never.

Go to black.

Scene Two

Same place. **Catherine** *is praying to the telephone.*

Catherine   Ring ring ring, please God, make him ring. Holy Mary Mother of God, I'll come back to the church, I'll do anything, make him ring now. Xavier, listen to me, pick up the fucking phone, please, I'm going off my head. I can't stand this. Why are you doing this to me? It's not fair. I'm getting an ulcer, you're making me ill. OK, I'm going to count to ten and then I'm going to phone you. If you haven't phoned by the time I've finished this joint I'm going to ring you, can you hear me? Just pick up the phone and speak to me. You could be dead for all I know, you could have had an accident or anything. Xavier, this is killing me.

Mary *comes in.* **Catherine** *looks at her.*

God, I hate him.

She picks up the phone and taps out a number.

Hola? Xavier, porfavor . . . Oh, right . . . It's Catherine . . . Catherine . . . I just wondered if he got my message because I tried to leave a number but the line went dead . . . Oh, I see . . . When? . . . Well, what time were you thinking he might . . . OK, could you tell him then, just tell him that I called, and if he could −

The line goes dead.

Hello? Hello?

Teresa *and* **Frank** *come in as she puts the phone down.*

Teresa   Did he call then?

Catherine   Yeah, yeah, he just rang, that was him –

Mary *turns and looks at her.* **Catherine** *refuses to catch her eye.*

Teresa   Where's Mike?

Mary   I've put him in a hot bath, he'd gone a bit blue.

Teresa   Look we've got to sort these flowers out, just look at the photos, will you? It'll take two minutes –

She hands the florist's book to **Mary**.

Catherine   Poor thing, he hasn't had a chance to get to the phone, there's been a flood in the restaurant, all the furniture's bobbing around in three feet of water, it's a disaster, but it'll come off the insurance, I suppose. So that's all right. Luckily.

Teresa   Oh dear. Frank, take those bags out to the car.

Catherine   I just hope he can make the funeral, I mean I hope it's all sorted out so he can get a flight tonight, otherwise, well, he won't, will he? Make the funeral.

Frank *picks up an armful of black plastic.*

Frank   Had he ever met your mother?

Catherine   He'd talked to her on the phone. Anyway, what's that supposed to mean? God, why does everyone in this house have to be so oblique and sneery, why can't anyone say what they mean?

Frank   Catherine, stop being so bloody paranoid –

Teresa   Frank. Bags. Car. Now.

Frank *puts the bags down.*

Frank   For Christ's sake, Teresa, I've just lifted a Bedford van out of a ditch, give me a break –

Teresa   Don't exaggerate –

Catherine   Mike's never met her either and no one's
complaining about him coming —

Teresa   OK, OK, so what did he say?

Catherine   Nothing. He said he'd phone back as soon as he
knew what was happening. That's what he said. Stop
interrogating me, OK?

Mary   I'll have number seventeen B.

She hands the book back to **Teresa**.

Teresa (*looking at the photo*)   She was allergic to lilies of the
valley, choose something else —

Mary   She's hardly going to start sneezing at her own
funeral, is she?

She takes the book again. **Frank** *grapples with the bags, one of which
bursts open.*

Frank   Oh, for fuck's sake!

Mike *comes in wrapped in a towel, clutching his clothes. He looks at
the assembled crowd.*

Teresa   Sorry Mike, d'you want to get dressed?

Mike   No no, I'm fine really, don't mind me.

Catherine   I bet you've used all the water —

Mary (*handing the florist's book to* **Teresa**)   Twenty-seven A,
not a lily in sight, absolutely no chance of impetigo, hives, or
nervous eczema for either mourners or deceased. Catherine,
you choose and then could you all leave us in peace for five
minutes?

Catherine   Why are you always trying to get rid of me?

Teresa   Oh don't start, Catherine. Choose your wreath for
heaven's sake —

She tries to give her the book.

Catherine   No, I always get this, 'Bugger off Catherine,
we don't want you here', well, what am I supposed to do?
Teresa's got Frank, you've got him, and what am I supposed

to do on my own? I don't want to sit in the living-room on my own while everyone else has smoochy secret conversations, it's not fair, not at a time like this, but if that's what you want —

She gets into the wardrobe and shuts the door.

Frank   Have you ever thought of laying off the drugs for a while, Catherine?

Catherine   Who asked you?

The phone rings. She dives out of the wardrobe and grabs it.

Hello? Xavier . . . God, how are you, where've you been? Did you get my . . . Oh, right . . . Oh . . . Right . . . What? . . . Oh. Well, couldn't you . . .

Long pause. She listens.

I don't think we should . . . maybe we should talk about this when I get back . . . Oh . . . OK, bye . . .

She puts the phone down. They all look at her. Awkward silence.

He can't come.

Teresa   Because of the flood?

Catherine   The what? Oh, no, well, yes, lots of things. Anyway, he's not coming.

Silence.

Mike   Are you all right?

Catherine   Yeah. Yeah. He said he'd ring back later.

She gets up.

So. What is there still to do? Shall we sort the drawers out? There's all the jewellery and stuff —

She goes to the dressing-table drawer and begins to rummage through it, taking things out haphazardly.

God, he's so funny sometimes, he's so apologetic. He was almost crying on the phone, you should have heard him. It's just a real drag he can't come, he's so lovely. Did I ever show you his photo? He's got beautiful teeth. I mean, he really, really wanted to come. It's just hopeless, you know, running a restaurant and everything, you never get any time off.

Mike   Maybe you'd like a cup of tea?

Catherine   I don't want any tea.

She takes a tin from the drawer and tries to open it.

Mike   Right. OK.

Mary   It's probably just as well he isn't coming. I mean, he wouldn't know anyone and it's a strange country and everything.

Catherine   Yes. It's probably just as well.

She hurls the tin across the room, narrowly missing **Frank**.

Frank (*ducking*)   Jesus –

Catherine   Fuck it!

Silence. She bursts into racking sobs.

I went to this counsellor – did I tell you this? – or a therapist or something and she said I had this problem and the problem was, I give too much, I just do too much for other people, I'm just a very giving person, and I never get any credit for any of it. I haven't even got any friends. I mean, I have but I don't like most of them, especially the women, and I try really hard, it's just I'm very sensitive and I get taken for a ride, nothing ever goes right, every time, I mean, every time it's the same – like with men. What is it with men? I mean, I don't have a problem with men or anything. I love men. I've been to bed with seventy-eight of them, I counted, so obviously there's not a problem or anything, it's just he didn't even apologize or anything and how can he say on the phone he doesn't want to see me any more? I mean, why now? Why couldn't he have waited? I don't know what to do, why does it always go wrong? I don't want to be on my own, I'm sick of people saying I'll be better off on my own, I'm not that sort of person, I can't do it. I did everything for him, I was patient and all the things you're supposed to be and people kept saying don't accept this from him, don't accept that, like, you know, when he stayed out all night, not very often, I mean once or twice, and everyone said tell him to fuck off, but how could I because what if he did? Because they all do, everyone I've ever met does, they all disappear and I don't know if it's me or what. I don't want to be on my own, I can't stand it, I know it's supposed to be great but I don't think it is. I can't help it, it's no good pretending, it's fucking lonely and I can't bear it.

She rushes out of the room. They look at each other. Silence. **Frank** *picks up the tin.*

Frank   She nearly had my head off.

Mary   Christ. I wonder what sort of therapist she went to. How could anyone in their right mind tell Catherine her problem was give give give?

She pours herself a whiskey.

Mike   Actually, it is, in a weird kind of way, she's trying to give you something all the time. It's usually inappropriate, that's all. I mean, she's obviously got some kind of problem.

Teresa   Yes, we don't need you to tell us that, thank you –

Mike   Sorry, she's just, I mean, pretty miserable and not very stable –

Teresa   Thank you, doctor –

Frank   Teresa –

Teresa   Well, I'm sick of people feeling sorry for her. It's very easy the first time you meet her, but if you put up with her year in year out, you just want to kill her –

She takes the glass from **Mary**.

Teresa   Give me some of that.

Frank   Teresa, don't drink whiskey, it makes you demented, you know that –

Teresa *knocks back the entire glass and grimaces.*

Teresa   Salt.

Frank   Don't drink it if it tastes of salt –

Teresa   I thought you were taking those bags to the car –

Mike   Maybe one of you should go and have a word with Catherine.

Teresa   How dare you walk in here and pontificate?

Frank   Put the bottle down, Teresa –

Mike   I just meant –

Mary   Don't get involved, Mike, please.

Mike   I'm just saying from an outsider's point of view, she gets a rough deal. I know you can't see it, because your tolerance has run out, but actually she's a mess and nobody really listens to her –

Teresa   Because she talks bollocks, that's why. I mean, this is rich, this is, coming from you, the man who's been two-timing his wife for the last five years telling us how to behave –

Frank   Teresa, what the hell's this got to do with anything? Stop it.

Teresa   No, why shouldn't I shout? Everyone else does in this house –

Frank   I never said you were shouting –

Teresa   Well, you're deaf then, because I am. Just answer me this, Mike –

Mary   Just ignore her –

Teresa   When are you going to do the decent thing? When are you going to leave your wife and marry my sister?

Frank   Oh, for Christ's sake, this is none of your business, Teresa –

Teresa   Well, it's about time someone asked –

Frank   But not you, and not now, OK?

Mike   It's very complicated.

Mary   You don't have to answer, Mike, it's OK. Teresa, can we stop this right here?

Mike   My wife's ill actually –

Teresa   Oh, very convenient.

Mary   She's got M.E.

Teresa   M.E. my arse.

Frank   Teresa, I'm warning you –

Teresa   What sort of illness is that?

Mary   Stop it!

Teresa   The sort of illness where you lie on the sofa for six months with a bit of a headache. It's not a proper illness. It's not a brain tumour. It's not as if she's got both her legs in traction. Let me tell you something, Mike.

Frank   I don't think you should tell anybody anything right at this moment –

Teresa   There's nothing wrong with your wife, Mike.

Mike   Well, there is actually.

Teresa   No. She knows you're having an affair so she thinks if she's ill, you won't leave her.

Frank   Sorry about this, Mike, like you said, it's the grief, you know –

Mike   Don't worry about it. I'm sorry, I shouldn't have stuck my oar in –

Frank   Teresa, come on now, you're talking shite, come and have a lie down.

Teresa   Actually, I'm not talking shite. Actually. I've done it. I've got ill so people would be nice to me. I used to do it to my ex-husband. Sometimes it's all that's left to you. You get ill for a reason. You do it so people won't go.

Frank   Teresa, I beg of you. Remember the last time. Three small gins, that's all. Took her bloody clothes off. In a car park.

Teresa   I was hot.

Mary   Give me the bottle. Now.

Teresa   Don't tell me what to do, and stop looking so bloody superior, because you've no cause –

Mary   His wife is ill. Genuinely ill. ME is real. It's not imaginary. OK?

Teresa   You see. We're our mother's daughters. Always take the man's side even when he's a complete pile of crap –

Frank   Teresa, that's enough –

Teresa   Just like with Dad.

Mary   Frank, get her out of here –

Teresa   Our father, Mike, hardly spoke at all during the forty-eight years he was married to our mother. D'you remember hearing him speak, Mary? D'you recall him ever uttering a word of encouragement, an endearment?

Mary   Teresa –

Teresa   He was like a professional mute. And fucking someone else for most of the time.

Frank   Right, that's it. Come on.

Teresa   D'you know what his last words were, Mike?

Mike   I don't, no.

Teresa   'Pass the mustard, Marjorie.'

Frank   That was George the Fifth –

Teresa   And she wasn't even called Marjorie. D'you understand?

Mary   For Christ's sake, this is all bollocks.

Teresa   Our mother's name was Violet and he said 'Pass the mustard, Marjorie'. I think that just about sums him up.

Mary   This is pure invention –

Teresa   How do you know? You weren't there. As usual. Never there in a crisis, not even your own. It's always someone else does the clearing up. Always me and Mum.

Frank   Teresa –

Teresa   All those years she never said a word against him. Dad was always right, it was a perfect marriage. We've no secrets, she used to say. For heaven's sake. Who was she trying to kid?

Mary   Teresa, please, I'm exhausted with this –

Teresa   No! Who was she trying to kid? Tell me.

Mary   I don't know. Herself. She was trying to kid herself. OK?

Frank   Mike, believe me, I'm on your side –

Teresa   She dyed her hair red, d'you remember that? Dad didn't even notice. Didn't say a word. I mean you could hardly miss it, it was a disaster, dogs ran away from her in the street –

Mary   He was being polite. He didn't want to hurt her –

Teresa   Stop putting a gloss on him, he didn't bloody care. We could have had three heads and he'd not have noticed. Our entire bloody lives spent making sure nothing ruffled his feathers. He used to laugh at the word stress. 'Stress,' he'd say, 'what a lot of rubbish.' He said he didn't know what it was. Of course he bloody didn't. We did it for him. We had the stress for him. We contorted ourselves. Literally, in your case –

Mary   I really don't want to get into this at the moment –

Teresa   I don't believe he didn't know. How could he not bloody know? I mean, he might have been mute but he wasn't blind for goodness' sake –

Mary   Yeah, well, it was a long time ago, let's just –

Teresa   No, let's not, let's not just pretend it never happened –

Mary   Nothing happened –

Teresa   Bloody hell, how can you not notice that someone's eight months pregnant?

Silence.

Frank   Who was eight months pregnant?

Silence.

Mary   Me.

Pause.

Teresa   She was fourteen.

Frank   Are you serious?

Mary   Yes. Anything else you'd like to know?

Mike   You never told me –

Mary   It was a long time ago. There's nothing to tell –

Teresa   What d'you mean, there's nothing to tell?

Mary   It's for me to tell or not. If I don't talk about it, that's my business. It didn't happen to you, it happened to me.

Teresa   Oh typical sollipsistic bollocks. No one exists but you. Have you any idea what Mum and I went through?

Mary   You went through nothing. What you went through was nothing, d'you understand me? No, I don't suppose you do, you stupid, unimaginative woman.

Frank   You're really excelling yourself today, Teresa. Although personally, I think your timing's a bit off. Much more effective if you'd waited till the funeral, and then got up and announced it to the congregation. You could have done it instead of the crappy Dylan Thomas poem. You'd have brought the house down.

Teresa   I'm tired of it. Why are we always trying to make life easier for you? Why should I carry your secrets? Why should she sail through her life getting pats on the back as if she'd never put a foot wrong?

Frank   It just strikes me as being a strange time to reveal it to the world, Teresa. I mean, it hardly qualifies as bereavement counselling –

Teresa   You don't know the half of it –

She picks up the bottle again.

Frank   If you take one more swig of that, your liver will explode –

Teresa   Hiding it all from Dad. It was ridiculous, but of course Mary was Goody Two Shoes, Snow White and Our Lady Of Lourdes all rolled into one as far as he was concerned, and we couldn't disabuse him of that convenient fiction, could we?

Mary   This is a novel told entirely from your point of view –

Teresa   Mum had to arrange everything, poor woman, all those lies about peritonitis and hospitals and God knows what –

Mary   She put her hand over my mouth when the pains started. I bet you've forgotten that bit –

Teresa   She did not. She found a lovely, Catholic family who brought him up in the true faith, while you got on with your true vocation of being the best at everything. No questions asked, never mention it again, it never happened, even Catherine doesn't know. Poor bloody Catherine, she's always complaining no one tells her anything, and she's right, no one ever did, no one ever will –

Mike   So there's a grown-up son somewhere –

Teresa   Mary this, Mary that, Mary's bloody homework, Mary's bloody exams. We used to creep around on tiptoes in case her precious brain cells got thrown off-kilter by sudden exposure to pop music or someone slamming the front door. And all it's done is make her think she's immune, with her breathtaking fucking arrogance –

Mary   This is a fabrication, this is a complete distortion of the truth –

Teresa   And you still think you're unassailable, you still bloody do –

Mary   You're drunk, I'm not listening to this –

She walks out furiously. **Mike** *hurries after her.*

Mike   I'll just, er . . . Excuse me a minute – Mary –

Frank   D'you know something, Teresa, you're not just embarrassing, you're really quite repulsive, when you're drunk. I'm going to give Mike some friendly advice: don't leave your wife. You don't want to marry into this lot. It's worse than the Borgias.

Teresa   Oh, shut up.

She starts to cry. Long silence. Tears stream down her face.

I've wanted to cry for three days.

She takes another swig of whiskey, sobbing.

The salt taste's gone.

Silence.

Say something, Frank.

Pause.

Frank   I've been awake for thirty-six hours.

Pause.

Teresa   You have a whole repertoire of silences, don't you?

Frank   Sorry?

Teresa   You've got a pissed-off one, and a resentful one, an I-hate-you-so-much-I'm-pretending-to-be-deaf one, and a worse one which is I-hate-you-so-much-I'm-pretending-to-be-foreign-and-I-don't-understand-anything-you're-saying. Your silences are the most eloquent thing about you. I can read them the way an eskimo reads snow.

Frank   Inuit.

Teresa   What?

Frank   Inuit. That's what they're called now. They don't like being called Eskimos any more.

Teresa   How do you know? How many Eskimos have you ever met?

Frank   Teresa, I'm shattered –

Teresa   You're always shattered.

Frank   What's that supposed to mean?

Teresa   You come home, stare at the wall and pass out. You can fall asleep over a supermarket trolley, I've seen you, you can even do it with your eyes open so you look like you're awake –

Frank   It's because you keep sending me to these bloody conferences, sales junkets, glee clubs . . . Fuck, I don't know what they are most of the time, half the time I don't even know where I am –

Teresa   I do not send you –

Frank   Well, you bloody go. You spend a week living on goose fat and pickled cabbage in some emerging democracy. You try persuading people who haven't seen a banana for six months that what they need is royal fucking jelly. Then try it for six months of every year and see how you feel. You wouldn't even make it as far as the supermarket to fall asleep. You'd probably be dead.

Teresa   It's not my fault if Albanians haven't got bananas, it's not my fault –

Frank   I never said that –

Teresa *is very, very drunk*.

Teresa   Why is it all my fault?

Frank   Teresa, what is it that you want from me? I can't do a thing right. What is it that I'm doing wrong?

Silence.

Why d'you do this to me?

Teresa Why do I do what? Oh he's so nice, Frank, isn't he, he's so good-natured. Well actually, I want to say, the minute he walks through his own front door, he's not nice, not remotely, he stops speaking in sentences, he just grunts, he's not the charming Frank you all think he is, he might as well be a hologram, it's a bloody nightmare, Frank, you're just like –

She stops. Pause.

Frank Just like who?

Teresa No one. Nothing.

She looks at him.

You said you were witty and entertaining. That's what you said.

Frank Oh, don't start all this again –

Teresa Witty and entertaining and five foot eleven. Hah!

Frank You said you were twenty-nine.

Teresa I did not say I was twenty-nine –

Frank Excuse me, oh, excuse me –

He takes a piece of paper from his wallet and reads.

Thoughtful, sexy, vegetarian woman, coming up thirty –

Teresa – seeks witty, entertaining man thirty to forty-five –

Frank You weren't coming up thirty –

Teresa And you weren't witty and entertaining.

Frank You didn't argue at the time.

Teresa Say something entertaining, then. Go on.

Frank Oh, for fuck's sake –

Teresa Well say something interesting, then. Tell me something new.

Pause.

Frank   I hated *Hannah and her Sisters*.

Teresa   What?

Frank   I hated it. I hate Woody Allen.

Teresa   *Hannah and her Sisters* was our first date.

Frank   I know.

Teresa   You said you loved it.

Frank   I was lying. I didn't get it. It wasn't funny.

Teresa   There's that bit where the man won't buy the paintings because they don't match his sofa. That's funny.

Frank   It's not. It's perfectly reasonable. You wouldn't buy, say, a big green and purple painting if you had a red sofa, would you? You'd scream every time you went into the living-room. You'd get migraine.

Teresa   That's not the point of the joke.

Frank   So what is the point, then?

Teresa   You've been pretending to like Woody Allen all these years. You've been lying. I've been married to a stranger –

Pause. She looks at him unsteadily.

Frank.

Frank   What?

Teresa   Are you having an affair?

Frank   What?

Teresa   Just tell me.

Frank *is bewildered.*

Frank   I'm not having an affair.

Teresa   Are you sure?

Frank   Oh hang on, let me rack my brains, it might have slipped my mind –

Teresa   I'm serious –

Frank   I'm not having an affair. I haven't got the energy –

Teresa   But if you ever. I mean. If you ever did have an affair you'd tell me, wouldn't you?

Frank   I thought that was the whole point of having an affair. You don't tell.

Teresa *punches him in the stomach. He gasps.*

Frank   I was joking. I was joking.

Teresa   You've got a horrible sense of humour.

Frank   I'm sorry. Put the bottle down. Come on, you've had enough. Sit down.

She hands him the bottle, tearfully. Pause. **Frank** *takes a deep breath.*

Teresa. During the course of my spectacularly indirect journey here from Dusseldorf, in between bouts with the mime artist, I did a bit of thinking. Two and a half days at a health food convention being harassed by people who do vitamin therapy according to star signs reminded me of what deep down I've known for some time. We sell utter crap.

Teresa   Frank –

Frank   No, hang on, let me finish. I know you believe in it. I know you do. But just answer this. Were your parents happy running a hardware shop? Running a business together?

Teresa   No, of course not.

Frank   So why did you think you would be?

Teresa   It's got nothing to do with my parents.

Frank *looks at her.*

Frank   Maybe later, when the funeral's out of the way, we could, you know . . .

Teresa   What?

Frank   I don't know. Maybe you should run the business and I should go into something else.

Teresa   Like what?

Frank   The thing is Teresa, I hate selling things. Or specifically, I hate selling things that people don't want and I don't believe in. I'm not cut out for it. I like a nice straight-forward transaction, you know? 'Good evening, two pints of bitter, and a rum and coke.' 'Certainly sir, ice and lemon? That'll be five pounds fifty, thank you.' End of transaction. Not, 'Can I interest you in a double port while we're at it? No? Well what about a set of toning tables, or cavity wall insulation?' I can't stand it, Teresa, it's driving me insane. I want to do something simple.

Teresa   Such as what?

Pause.

Frank   A pub. I want to run a pub.

Teresa   You want to run a pub?

Frank   I've seen one for sale just outside Ripon.

Teresa *staggers to her feet.*

Teresa   A pub! I don't believe you –

Catherine *walks in.*

Catherine   What's going on?

Frank   Nothing's going on, I'm trying to have a conversation with Teresa –

Teresa   I think I'm going to be sick. No, don't come near me. A pub, you must be out of your mind –

Frank   Teresa –

Teresa   Don't touch me. A pub, a pub for God's sake –

She goes out. Crashing noises from outside the room. Swearing. **Frank** *lies back on the bed, exhausted.*

Catherine   Oh God.

She jumps on to the bed next to **Frank**.

I'm so depressed.

Frank   Yeah, well, you know, it's a depressing business.
Dying and what not.

Silence.

Catherine   Frank?

Frank   What?

Catherine   Am I unattractive?

Frank   I'm sorry?

Catherine   D'you think I'm pretty?

Frank   Of course you're pretty. Look Catherine, I'm
exhausted, I'm talked out, I'm sorry.

Pause.

Catherine   I'm very pretty. I'm good fun. I'm a very
special person. That's what Carmen, my therapist, said. I'm
a brilliant cook. So why did he leave me?

Frank   Jesus, Catherine, I don't know. People leave each
other. You'll get over it. I have to go and talk to Teresa.

Catherine   She's probably being sick. That's what she
usually does if she drinks. What am I going to do?

Frank   About what?

Catherine   Xavier.

Frank   Catherine, I've no advice to give you. I'm a
middle-aged man with a health food business I don't believe
in, and a normally teetotal wife who's taken to the bottle. I
could say, have some ginseng tea, eat organic vegetables and
learn to love yourself, but it's all a lot of bollocks.

Catherine   I have to get back to him, I can't bear it. I have
to see him. I mean, this is the real thing, I know it is, so I can't
just give in can I? . . . I can't bear it —

She puts her head in his lap. He looks at her as if she's an unexploded bomb. He tries to move away. She puts her arms round him.

Frank   OK, OK, OK, that's enough, Catherine, take it easy —

Catherine   I need a hug.

He pats her awkwardly.

Frank   There you go.

Catherine   That's not a hug.

Frank   Teresa'll give you a hug.

Catherine   How can she, with her head down the toilet?

She grips him tightly.

Frank   Catherine, get off my leg —

Catherine   It's OK, you're family —

Frank   Exactly —

Catherine   Hold me, Frank, I'm so bloody lonely. What am I going to do? I just need a bit of a hug, that's all —

Frank   Catherine, I'm very flattered but steady on, eh, we don't want to —

She kisses him, immediately pulls away and jumps off the bed.

Catherine   I wasn't trying to seduce you or anything —

Frank   Catherine, you're a bit crazy at the moment, OK —

Catherine   Oh, typical —

Frank   No, I mean, it's understandable, look at Teresa. If I were you I'd phone this Pepe now, and tell him to eff off, just say 'I'm sorry, Pepe, my mother's just died, I don't need this, take a hike — '

Catherine   He's not called Pepe —

Frank   Or whatever. Jose —

Catherine   Oh, for fuck's sake, all I wanted was a bit of affection. A bit of support. That's all I was asking for. I wasn't asking you to marry me and bear my children. What is it with men? Why d'you always have to misread the signals? God, you make me sick —

Mary *and* **Mike** *come in.* **Mary** *is carrying a tin box.*

Mary   I know you're drawn to this room like moths to a flame, but believe me, I've had enough of all of you. If anyone rings I'll let you know —

Catherine   I was going anyway —

She goes out. **Frank** *gets up.*

Frank   I'm worried about her. I'm serious — she needs six months in a secure unit, she's completely — anyway, I'd better go and sort Teresa out —

He goes. **Mary** *sits on the bed and opens the box. She sifts through papers.*

Mike   I'm sorry.

Mary   What about?

Mike   Everything.

She rifles through the tin.

Why d'you need his birth certificate?

Mary   I'm putting my name on a register, so that if he's looking for me, he'll find me. I don't even know what he looks like. I have to make him up. I sit on tubes looking at twenty-five-year-old boys, and I think, maybe that's him. Ever since he went I've been looking for him, but he's like ether, I can't get hold of him.

She unfolds a piece of paper.

Oh, thank God. Thank God it's still here. Here he is. Oh, look. Patrick. Patrick James. My boy. I wanted to call him Heathcliff. I was fourteen. I still thought life was a novel. (*She reads.*) 'Sex: boy. Name: Patrick James. Weight: six pounds four ounces.' This is all I've got left of him.

She looks round the room.

This will all be gone soon. All this furniture, all this stuff. The room will go probably. It'll disappear into the sea. And this is all I want to take from the house. This is the only thing I want to salvage. So I can prove he's mine.

She puts the paper in her bag. Puts her hand on her stomach, and goes to the mirror. Looks at herself sideways.

It's a strange feeling being pregnant. You wake up one morning and you feel so absolutely other.

She looks at him.

Mike   Mary, I think, you know, you're jumping the gun here —

Mary   I need a real child, not a ghost one. What are you going to do? Are you sticking with me or walking away?

Mike   If you are pregnant, *if* you are, of course, I mean of course I won't walk away, I just don't think it's — look, I know Charlie Morgan's in the Betty Ford clinic —

Mary   You could always sue him. Everyone else is.

Mike   Look. I know you want a child, I accept that. I know you're furious with me for having a vasectomy —

Mary   Five years and you never mentioned it, that's what I can't —

Mike   I don't want a child, Mary! I don't want a child. I can't want one just because you do. Love and paternity aren't indivisible in my mind. When I say I love you it means I like you, I want to be with you, I want to go to bed with you, it means all sorts of things but it doesn't necessarily mean three children and Sainsbury's every Saturday for the next thirty years —

Mary   No, you've already got that —

Mike   I can't help what happened before I met you! You might not like what I'm telling you, but I can't lie to make you feel better. I never wanted kids in the first place. They happened and now I love them but I don't want any more. It's not because I'm cold or selfish — at least no more than anyone else is – it's that I feel sucked dry by what people need from me – patients, Chrissie, the children. You're where I come to be equal, I come to you because you're not asking to be healed. Some people aren't paternal. It's not a crime. I'm one of them. If you're a woman and you take care of your own fertility, nobody argues. Well, I've taken care of mine. I didn't have a vasectomy because Chrissie's ill, I had it for me.

Silence.

But obviously, you know, if you *are* pregnant, I'll stick by you.

Mary   Well, hey. That makes me feel a whole lot better.

Pause.

Jesus. Oh, Jesus, what a mess. Bring back the days when we had no choice in the matter.

Mike   Well you did have a choice. You chose me.

Mary   Oh choice shmoice. Have you seen what's on offer out there? Tiny little trainspotters in grey shoes, maniacs, alcoholics, men who wear their underpants for a week.

There's a knock at the door.

Go away.

Catherine *comes in.*

Catherine   D'you know what she's gone and done?

Mary   I don't know and I don't care.

Catherine   I'll kill her –

Frank *comes in.*

Frank   Look, I'm sorry, I know you're trying to get a bit of peace –

Mary   Oh don't mind about us, please –

Frank   The thing is, Teresa's arranged for your mother to come back, that's all.

Pause.

Mary   Sorry, I'm obviously in the grip of an aural hallucination. Say that again.

Catherine   The night before. She's coming back here. The night before the funeral. Tonight.

Mary   What, in her coffin?

Catherine   No she's coming on foot, what d'you think?

Mary   Apart from anything else, where are we going to put her?

Frank   In here, this is her room.

Mary   I'm sleeping in here. I can't sleep next to my dead mother. For Christ's sake.

Mike   We can go to a hotel —

Frank   You can have it open or closed, it's up to you.

Catherine   She's dead. I don't want to see her dead face.

Teresa *appears in the doorway, drunk and dishevelled.*

Teresa   You should see her, it's important, and then you'll know she's dead —

Catherine   She's been in a fridge for four days, of course she's bloody dead —

Teresa   Well, I'm sorry, she's coming home, I've arranged it and that's that and it's no good saying why didn't I ask you because you weren't here to ask. She's coming home to spend her last night in her own bedroom. And that's the end of the story. The end. Full stop. *Finito. La fin.*

She sways precariously.

Frank . . .

Frank   What?

Teresa   I've had far too much to drink . . .

Go to black.

Scene Three

Same room, early next morning. The coffin is there on a low trestle.
Teresa *is dressed for the funeral, talking on the phone.* **Catherine**
is sitting in her dressing gown, staring at the coffin.

Teresa So when you say 'even later', you mean what? . . .
I see . . . No, of course . . . I understand . . . Could you ring
as soon as – thank you . . . Bye . . .

She looks at **Catherine***, looks at her watch.*

They must be snowed in.

Catherine Who?

Teresa The men who carry the coffin. Funeral operatives,
he calls them. They still haven't shown up for work. He's
trying to find some replacements. I wish I knew what he
meant, I mean we don't want amateurs doing it. It's
supposed to be dignified. You can't just get anyone in.

Catherine *says nothing. She's staring at the coffin.*

Why don't you get dressed, or are you thinking of going like
that?

Catherine It's tiny, isn't it?

Teresa *looks.*

Teresa She was only small.

Catherine Not as small as that.

Teresa She must have been. They don't fold them up.

Pause.

Catherine D'you think they make them to measure?

Teresa I suppose they must.

Catherine I suppose so. Yeah. I mean babies' coffin's are
tiny, aren't they? They're about this big.

Teresa They'd have to be. Otherwise they'd rattle
around.

Catherine   Mmmm . . . Unless you used loads of bubble wrap.

Teresa   If you want to look at her, you just have to undo a little screw at the top. They gave me a wee screwdriver.

Silence.

I don't want to, do you?

Catherine   Not really, no.

Pause. She turns away from the coffin.

I'm so depressed. I can't change my flight.

Teresa   Forget him. He's a bastard.

Catherine   How do you know?

Teresa   You've never had a boyfriend who isn't. You don't go about it the right way.

Catherine   There was that nice Swiss one. He was all right. Did you ever meet him? He was gorgeous, I felt just like Heidi.

Teresa   I knew Frank was the right man for me straight away. Because I chose him. I got forty-seven replies. I whittled them down and chose the most compatible.

Catherine   Yeah, but the thing is . . .

Teresa   What?

Catherine   At the end of the day you still landed up with Frank.

Teresa   We're very, very happy actually. We're a perfect match. Because we went about it in the right way –

Catherine   D'you know who he reminds me of?

Teresa   Don't say it.

Catherine   He does though, doesn't he? It must be a bit depressing. You go through all the palaver of whittling out the dross and you end up married to your dad.

Mary *comes in, dressed for the funeral. She looks white and drawn.*

Teresa Oh, there you are. You look lovely.

Pause. **Mary** *looks at the coffin.*

How was the hotel?

Mary Fine.

Teresa *watches her looking at the coffin.*

Sorry. It's a bit of a shock. Brings you up a bit short, doesn't it . . . ?

Catherine Everyone's snowed in. There's no one to carry it —

Teresa That's no reason to still be in your dressing gown —

Catherine OK, OK, I'll get dressed, I'm going, don't worry.

She goes out. **Mary** *looks round the room, obviously searching for something.*

Teresa I'm sorry about yesterday.

Mary Forget it.

Teresa I shouldn't drink.

Mary No. You shouldn't.

She sits on the bed and takes the green tin from underneath. Begins to look through it. **Teresa** *looks at her sharply.*

Teresa Where did you find that?

Mary At the back of the airing cupboard. Why?

Teresa When?

Mary Yesterday. I wanted the copy of his birth certificate.

Teresa *snatches the tin from her.*

Teresa It's not in here.

Mary *is bewildered.*

Mary I know it's not. I took it out. I was just wondering if there was anything else —

Teresa Like what?

Mary I've no idea, adoption papers. For goodness' sake, what's the matter with you?

Teresa It's just old gas bills and bus tickets, you know what she was like, she could never throw anything away –

Mary I just want to see if there's anything else about Patrick –

Teresa There's not, I've looked.

Mary Teresa, this is ridiculous, I'm not in the mood, give me the tin.

Teresa *holds on to it grimly, unable to think of a response.*

Please.

Teresa I'll give it to you later. After the funeral. OK?

Mary Why can't I have it now?

Teresa We'll sort it out later, OK.

Mary Sort what out? Give me the tin, for goodness' sake –

She makes a grab for it. A tussle.

Teresa I told you, I'll give it to you later –

More tussling.

Mary What is it?

Teresa Nothing!

Tussle gets more violent.

Mary Give me the bloody tin!

They fight. **Teresa** *manages to hang on. She sits down with the tin.*

Teresa, what the fuck is this about?!

Teresa Nothing. Nothing. I'll tell you later –

Mary Tell me now.

Teresa I can't.

Pause.

Mary It's about Patrick, isn't it?

Teresa *looks stricken. Pause.*

Teresa There're some cuttings in here about him. Newspaper cuttings.

Mary You know where he is?

Pause.

Where is he?

Pause.

Teresa He's dead.

Silence.

I'm sorry. I wanted to tell you. I would have. I would have. I'm sorry. I told Mum, but she said no, and then . . . I mean, and then it was . . . I mean, the moment had passed —

Silence.

Mary What happened to him?

Teresa Some cliffs gave way. Just outside Whitby. Him and another boy. Father Michael told us.

Frank (*off*) Teresa! What's happened to my trousers?

Teresa I meant to tell you, but when? When could we have told you?

Mary When it happened. Why didn't you tell me when it happened?

Teresa (*offering her the tin, gently*) They're in an envelope marked medical cards. The cuttings.

Frank (*off*) Teresa!

Mary Go to him. Don't let him come in here.

Teresa Mary, I'm sorry —

Mary Go.

She goes. The lighting changes to the bluish-green glow. Faint sound of big band music in the distance. **Vi** *appears in the open doorway. Her hair is now completely white. She looks at the coffin.*

Vi   Open the box.

She goes over to the coffin. **Mary** *says nothing.*

It's open. Look.

She lifts the top section of the lid and looks.

A bloody old woman. I don't recognize her. A bloody old woman in green eyeshadow. Green. They call this dignity, apparently. Green frosted eyeshadow.

She shuts the lid. Closes her eyes and sways gently to the music.

I just want one last dance before I go . . .

Mary *watches her for a while. Empties the stuff out of the tin. Finds the envelope, takes out cuttings, looks at them in bewilderment.*

Mary   Nineteen eighty . . . Nineteen eighty . . . Why didn't you tell me?

Vi *stops dancing. Pause.*

Vi   It seemed right at the time. You were doing your finals.

Silence.

Mary   I've been waiting for him all these years. I've been waiting for him to turn up and claim me.

Vi   Don't become one of those women who blame. Don't be a victim. It's beneath you.

Mary   You should have told me. I could have stopped dreaming.

Vi   I know. I know that now.

Mary   You made me give him away because it was embarrassing. For you. Not for me.

Vi   I wanted you to do well. I didn't want you to be trapped. I did it for you.

Mary   I look at this patient of mine. This twenty-year-old boy lying in a hospital bed, completely blank, no memory of anything at all, just an empty vessel. And all I see is Patrick. Full of memories that I didn't put there, that someone else filled him with. And I think, did I give him anything? Is there some part of him that's still mine? Maybe he smiles like me. Maybe he walks like me. Maybe he doesn't. You made me obsessed.

Vi I did it for the best. I've told you that. I did the best I could.

Mary You've pretended all these years that it never happened. Well, it did. Nothing disappears without trace. You wouldn't let me bury him. You left me haunted.

Vi I thought nothing could shake you. I was wrong.

Pause.

Mary Last night, I dreamt I was in a fishmonger's. On the slab, there was a box. It seemed to be full of chickens. Trussed. I couldn't be sure. 'Are they chickens?' I said. He pulled back the sacking and they weren't chickens but babies. Dead trussed babies, no bigger than my hand. When I woke up, blood. I'm not pregnant. I never was. Everything's dead. I can't bear it. I can't hold on to anything.

Vi Despair is the last refuge of the ego.

Pause.

I got that out of the *Reader's Digest*.

Pause.

Mary I'm in freefall. I opened a door and stepped out into thin air.

Vi I never knew how you felt. I never know how you felt about anything. You thought your feelings were too rarefied to share with me. You cut me out. You looked straight through me. You shared nothing with me, not a joke, not a smile that wasn't patronizing, you never let me in, you never let me know you. This stony punishment all these years, wanting me to be better than I am, always your mother, always responsible, always to blame. How could I apologize, when you wouldn't give me the room?

Silence.

Mary   I'm sorry.

Pause.

What was it like? The last few months?

Vi   It's been a long time since you asked me a proper question. It's been a long time since you allowed me to know more than you.

Mary   Tell me what it felt like.

Vi   Like I had holes in my brain. Frightening. Huge rips. I'd not recognize people. You just think, where am I? What's going on? And then you don't know what you mean when you say 'I'. It doesn't seem to mean anything.

Mary   You always still looked like you. Like essence of you. The way you moved your hands sometimes. Your laugh.

Vi   Some things stay. Some things are in your bones. Songs. Babies. I was very keen on babies. Dogs. People's hair. Dancing. I wanted to dance. Usually in what Teresa called inappropriate places. Like the garden.

Mary   But who did you feel like? Who are you if you take your memories away?

Vi   I felt like I'd gone away. Like I'd broken up into islands and in between was just a terrible muddle of old songs and odd names drifting by, men I vaguely recognized. I felt like a cut-up thing. But sometimes the pieces would float to the surface, drift back together, and there I was, washed ashore from a pitch black sea of nothing. Me. Still me. I'm still here.

Pause.

Forgiving someone's just like throwing a switch.

Mary   Is it?

Vi   It's just a decision. And afterwards you're free.

Pause.

I've done it.

Mary Have you?

Vi I forgave your father. And now I'll forgive you. But it's time I went.

She goes to the mirror and looks at herself.

Yes. I think it is.

Mary Mum. Don't go just yet —

Vi *gives her one last look before she goes.* **Mary** *puts her head in her hands and cries.* **Teresa** *and* **Frank** *come in.*

Teresa Frank, get the Rescue Remedy.

Frank She needs a bloody drink.

She takes hold of her.

Teresa Mary, pull yourself together, you've got a funeral to go to. Frank, she needs Rescue Remedy, now —

Frank *goes out.*

Mary I'm past rescuing —

Teresa Take some of these —

She tries to give her some tablets.

Mary What are they?

Teresa Aconite, it's just a matter of —

Mary It's not just a matter of anything, it's my life! Stop trying to make it little and solvable, stop trying to sort it out with vitamin pills!

Teresa They're not vitamin pills —

Mary There's no cure.

Frank *comes in with* **Mike**. **Mike** *goes to her.*

Frank Rescue Remedy. Duty-free Vodka. Take your pick.

Mike Are you all right?

Mary I'm tired, I didn't sleep.

Frank   I read somewhere the other day that if you eat a whole lettuce before you go to bed, it has pretty much the same effect as a Mogadon.

Mary   Well I'm torn now. I don't know whether to have a Caesar salad or cut my throat.

She takes the Rescue Remedy from **Frank***, and downs the lot.*

Teresa   No, no, you just need a few drops –

Mary   There you are, I feel better already. Suddenly life makes sense, suddenly my mother's not dead, I am actually pregnant, in fact it's triplets. Suddenly there is meaning where there was none before. Suddenly I'm Princess Michael of fucking Kent.

She sits down, exhausted. Silence.

Teresa   Pregnant?

Mary   A fantasy.

Mike   Sorry?

Mary   I thought I was pregnant, but I'm not. It was a phantom. You obviously caught Charlie Morgan on a good day.

Teresa (*desperately*)   Oh, why don't you two have a baby? Why don't you? Leave your wife and have a baby with Mary –

The door opens and **Catherine** *appears, in a very short skirt.*

Catherine   Hi. What d'you think?

They look at her in confusion.

Teresa   What?

Catherine   The outfit. What d'you think?

Frank   Sorry?

Catherine   Do I look all right?

Silence.

Frank   Very nice.

Teresa It's half-way up your bottom.

Catherine It's the only one I've got. Mary, d'you like it?

Mary Apart from the fact you can see your ovaries, it's fine —

The phone rings and **Frank** *picks it up.*

Frank Hello? . . . Oh, Jesus wept . . . And what? You've got what? . . . I don't believe this . . . Can we what? I beg your pardon? . . . I'm sorry? Well, I mean, I suppose if . . . Right, OK, OK, thanks, OK.

He puts the phone down.

He's on his way. He says, do we have any gentleman who can give him a hand? Taking the coffin out to the hearse.

Pause.

Mike Fine, right, OK, no problem, absolutely.

Frank I think he said it's a bit difficult for him because he's got a *plastic hand*. Is my hearing going or what?

Teresa I'm afraid not, no.

Catherine *is staring at the coffin.*

Catherine Did you open the lid?

Teresa No.

Catherine It's so weird.

Teresa What is?

Catherine It's weird she's in this box. I mean, I can't imagine it.

Frank I don't think you're supposed to.

Teresa You can't help it though, can you? Actually, if you think about it, it could be anyone in here. We'd never know the difference.

Catherine We'll never see her again. And she's so close. She had such a nice face.

Pause.

I wish she wasn't dead.

Mike   Maybe we could all do with a drink.

He begins to pour whiskey for everyone. **Teresa** *puts her arm round* **Catherine**.

Catherine   I'm all right. I'll be OK. I'll be OK. I will.

Mike *hands out drinks. Awkward silence.*

Frank   Whoops. Nearly said cheers.

Silence.

So. Here we are then.

He looks at his watch. Then at the coffin.

I presume it's a veneer, is it?

Teresa   What?

Frank   The coffin. Chipboard and veneer.

They all look at the coffin.

Mary   Well, you know, we were going for the jewel encrusted mother of pearl but we thought this would burn better.

Silence.

Sorry.

Frank   You can get do-it-yourself coffins now, apparently. Made of cardboard.

Mary   Oh, good.

Mike   Something to do in the long winter evenings. Build your own coffin.

Sound of a car horn from outside. **Mary** *goes to the window.*

Mary   That'll be him.

Mike   Right. OK. Shall we, er . . . Frank?

Frank   God. Right. I'll take this end, shall I?

He takes one end of the coffin.

Mike   Keep your back straight —

They lift.

Frank   I'll go backwards, or would you rather?

Mike   No, no, I'm fine — can someone hold the door?

Teresa *does so. They manoeuvre the coffin.* **Catherine** *starts to laugh madly.*

Catherine   Poor Mum. Even her funeral's a cock-up.

Mike   Pull her round to the right a bit — the right —

Frank   Mind that bit of carpet — whoops, nearly . . . that's it . . .

They go out.

(*Off.*) To me, to me —

The women pull on coats and gloves, etc.

Mary   Just check your phone's not in your bag will you?

Teresa   I've checked.

Catherine   I look ridiculous, don't I?

Mary   You don't. You look fine.

Catherine   I didn't hate her really.

Mary   I know that. We all know that. She didn't hate you either.

Pause.

Catherine   D'you remember, when Dad was out sometimes, she used to get us up in the middle of the night and give us crisps and ice cream soda?

Mary   And she'd have a Dubonnet and lemonade. God, I'd forgotten about that.

Teresa   She called it a girls' night in.

Catherine   We were all sleepy in our pyjamas, and she'd put on Nat King Cole.

Pause.

Mary   She must have been lonely. I never thought of that.

Silence.

Catherine   I put a hip flask in my bag in case we need it.

Teresa   I think I'll pass on that, if you don't mind.

Mary   Got tissues?

Teresa   Yes.

Frank *and* **Mike** *come in.*

Frank   Are we set?

Teresa   I think so. Shall we go, then? Are we ready?

Mary   You go on ahead. I'll be out in a minute.

Teresa   Come with us, Catherine. Come on.

Frank, **Teresa** *and* **Catherine** *go out.* **Teresa** *with her arm around* **Catherine**. *Silence.* **Mary** *and* **Mike** *look at each other.*

Mary   I think maybe that French guy was right.

Mike   Sorry?

Mary   The one who said water was like magnetic tape. My mother's the ghost in the machine. She goes through us like wine through water. Whether we like it or not. Nothing ends entirely.

Mike   What are you going to do?

Mary   Can you live a rich life without a child?

Mike   You know you can.

Pause.

Mary   Yes. I suppose so.

Pause.

I'm going to ask you something, Mike. I'm going to ask it once and I'll never ask it again. Leave your wife and come with me.

Pause.

Mike I think . . . I don't think we should talk about this now. Maybe we should talk about it after the funeral . . .

Mary I'm not asking you to talk about it. Take your chance, Mike.

Pause.

Mike (*almost a whisper*) Maybe afterwards we could . . .

She goes to the window. He looks at her helplessly. She looks out of the window.

Mary This snow's never going to stop. Everything frozen in its tracks. Everything cancelled.

Teresa (*off*) Mary!

Mary I've hated winter all my life. Ice on the windows, dark at three in the afternoon. Sea fret freezing the hairs in your nostrils. I've hated the stasis, the waiting for spring.

Teresa (*off*) Mary!

She turns to **Mike**.

Mike What are you going to do?

Mary Learn to love the cold.

They go out. As they leave, the lights dim to gold and blue. The curtains billow into the room and a flurry of snow drifts in. Nat King Cole plays faintly in the distance.

Fade down lights. Curtain.

Five Kinds of Silence

Five Kinds of Silence was first broadcast on BBC Radio 4 on 29 July 1996, with the following cast:

Billy	Tom Courtenay
Mary	Sue Johnston
Susan	Julia Ford
Janet	Lesley Sharp

Other roles were played by Alice Arnold, Stephen Critchlow, Mark Lambert, Caroline Strong, Patience Tomlinson, Tracey Wiles

Directed by Jeremy Mortimer

Characters

Billy	*Narrative 1* is the more objective, dispassionate voice of Billy as observer, describing events remembered
	Narrative 2 is the more disjointed, immediate voice of Billy, re-creating events, acting them out in an urgent present
Mary	Billy's wife
Janet	their daughters
Susan	
Policeman	
Policewoman	
Police Inspector	female
Police Photographer	non-speaking
Lawyer	female
Lawyer 2	male
Psychiatrist	male
Psychiatrist 2	female

The action of the play takes place in Burnley in 1995.

Billy (*Narrative 1*)   One night I dreamt I was a dog. The
moon was out, I could smell it. Ice white metal smell. I could
smell the paving stones, wet, sharp. The tarmac road made
my dog teeth tingle, it was aniseed, rubber, and then the
lampposts, glittering with smells, they were, studded with
jewels of sharp sweet spice, wood, metal, meat. And the stars
pierced my dog nose like silver wires. A woman came out of
her house, sickly the smell of her, rotten, she smelt of armpits
and babies and fish and a hundred other things screaming at
me like a brass band. I knew what she'd had for her tea. I
knew she was pregnant. I could smell it. She didn't look at
me, walked straight on by, thought I was just a dog. I
laughed a quiet dog laugh, you think I'm a dog but I'm Billy,
I'm me. The night smells of soot and frost and petrol and
beer. I'm at my own door now. I don't need to see it, it comes
to meet me, a cacophony, the smells are dancing towards me,
the smells of home. I'm inside the house now. Hot citrus smell
of electric light. My wife, my daughters, stand up as I come
into the room. Oh, home, the smells I love, all the tiny,
shimmering background smells, and the two I love the most,
the two smells that fill the room like a siren. One of them is
fear: burning tyres, vinegar, piss. And the other one is the
smell of blood, matted in Mary's hair. I gave her a good
kicking before I went out.

Title music.

Scene One

Family home. Living-room.

*A TV quiz programme chirps in the background. A rifle shot rings out.
Silence. The TV tinkles on.*

Janet   Is he dead?

Susan   He's stopped moving, Janet.

Janet   I'm frightened he's not dead.

Door opens, **Mary** *comes in, bewildered.*

Mary   What've you done, Susan?

Susan   We had to kill him Mum.

Janet   He's moving. I can see him moving.

Susan   He's dead.

Janet   Give me the gun. Best be sure.

Gun being reloaded.

Mary   What are you doing?

Janet   Finish him off. Don't want him to suffer.

She takes aim, a second shot rings out.

Billy (*Narrative 1*)   No need to do it twice. I was dead the first time. Like shooting a dog in its kennel. They got me when I was down, see. I didn't stand a chance. Bitches. It wasn't a fair fight.

Janet   We should have done it years ago.

Silence.

Mary   I'll call the police then. Shall I?

Susan   We need a drink.

Janet   We'll drink his whiskey. We'll drink all of it.

Susan   Later we'll get the police.

Mary   He looks nice like that. Lying there nice and still. In his red shirt.

Susan   It's blood. The shirt was white.

Mary   Still. He looks nice and neat. Nice and tidy. He'd be pleased. He never liked mess.

Janet   Why doesn't he close his eyes?

Susan *pours out whiskey.*

Susan   Drink.

They drink, gulping it down. Silence. The TV tinkles with music and canned laughter.

Janet   Susan?

Susan   What?

Janet   Is his eye flickering? Can you see it?

Susan   He's dead.

Janet   Look. There, there.

Susan   We killed him. We had to do it. Nothing's flickering.

Janet   If he comes back to life I'll top myself.

Scene Two

Billy (*Narrative 2*)   Wet sheets, steam, cold slapping against my face, I'm hiding. Suddenly someone's here. Big white arms. Big boney hands that do things I don't like. Punch me. Other stuff. What? What other stuff? She's big, huge. Veins in her white legs, like blue knotted ropes, rotten cheese. Ugly, I hate looking at them. Muscles at the back of the knees, bulging, yellow skin on the heels. Clatter of what? Clogs on a hard floor. Noise that splits my head in two, hot metally taste in my mouth. Crack goes the bone of my head. Stars float, I'm laughing, ha ha, hit me again if you want, I won't cry, I never cry, me. Crack, I slip in the wet. Crack goes another bone, elbow maybe. The side of my head burns. Out of my mouth comes a noise like kittens make when you drown them. But no, I'm laughing that's what I'm doing, I don't care me, if you cut my arms and legs off, if you hit me with the belt till my skin peels off I won't cry, I'd just laugh, right. But when I get bigger I'll bloody kill you.

Scene Three

Family home. Living-room.

Police sirens wailing. Heavy boots clumping through house. Male voices. General background activity, hubbub. The **Policeman** *is quite gentle, not at all aggressive, but slightly bewildered. The women's voices are flat and lifeless.*

Susan   We did it. My sister and I did it. Mum was in another room.

Mary   Can I get you a cup of tea, officer?

Policeman   You two shot your father?

Mary   Is he dead?

Policeman   They're taking him away now.

Mary   But is he dead?

Janet   We shot him twice. Was that enough?

Susan   Will we go to prison?

Policeman   Was it an accident?

Janet   We don't mind if we go to prison. Do we Susan?

Susan   We don't mind. No.

Mary   Just tell us if he's dead.

Policeman   It seems that way.

Susan   Are you sure?

Policeman   It's not official.

Janet   I told you, I told you, I saw his eye flickering.

Policeman   Was there a reason for shooting him? You must have had a reason.

All   We don't want to talk about that.

Policeman   Something's gone on hasn't it?

Mary   Things have been . . . quite tense recently.

Susan   Tense, yes.

Janet   What with his fits.

Mary   Six a day sometimes.

Susan   Our nerves have been bad.

Mary   Never knew when a fit would take him.

Policeman   He was having fits, so you shot him? Is that what you're saying?

Mary   He wasn't . . . he wasn't an easy man.

Susan   He was a difficult man.

Policeman   And that's your reason is it?

Silence.

Is it?

Janet (*very quietly*)   We don't want to talk about it. If you don't mind.

Scene Four

Billy (*Narrative 1*)   I'm in bed, it's pitch dark, I'm holding my knees to my chest. Icy, icy cold, you can't sleep for it, not even with your coat on and your boots. There's shouting along the landing, banging, same as every night, he's drunk. She's screaming at him.

(*Narrative 2*)   You bastard you useless bloody bastard, you're no bloody good to me, and he's roaring at her like a bull in an abattoir, no words, too drunk for that. Under the covers now, me, stop it stop it but I can hear them I know them. I've seen them biting and tearing and heads banged off walls teeth fly blood spurts. You stupid drunk pig! They're staggering, three steps this way, three steps that, one two three, one two three. Wood splinters. You stupid blind drunk fuck pig!

(*Narrative 1*)   I hear him fall, feel his bones, his blind head hits each stair, sinews tear and snap. She says get out, you're no good to anyone. I'm out of bed now, running downstairs.

The front door's open, she's trying to throw him into the street but he's holding her round the throat and she screams like this, agghhh, like a banshee. I don't want my mother to make noises like that, so I kick her, I don't know why but I do. He's on his hands and knees in the street, there's frost on the ground glittering. He gets up and falls over because he's drunk and he's blind and his hands are stretched out, he wants someone to help him. Sounds come from him, there's snot and tears.

(*Narrative 2*)   Bitch he says, bitch. Stupid blind bastard, stop it, stop crying Dad, you mustn't ever cry, I don't like looking at you when you do that, I don't like hearing you. I'm glad when she slams the door. She punches my head, bang, what are you doing up? It's cold upstairs Mum, it's pitch black dark, it's like being blind I don't want to go blind like my dad I don't want to go blind, she pulls me by my arm, twists with both hands like she's wringing out washing. Don't be so bloody soft, she says, don't be so bloody soft.

(*Narrative 1*)   I don't like to think about him out there in the dark, banging into things. I don't like to think about it. So I don't.

Scene Five

Police cell.

Door being locked. **Janet** *being led in.*

Janet   Is this a cell?

Policewoman   Yes.

Janet   It's beautiful.

Policewoman   You should try and get some sleep.

Janet   I could live here.

Policewoman   I'll take your belt.

Janet   You're not to lock the door.

Policewoman   I know.

Janet   I'm on anti-depressants.

Policewoman   I know.

Janet   If you lock the door I'll panic. I've never slept on my own.

Policewoman   How old are you Janet?

Janet   Thirty-four. I've always slept with my sister.

Policewoman   Even when you went on holiday?

Janet   We've never been on holiday. We've never been anywhere.

Policewoman   The door will be open. I'll be right outside.

Janet   We had to do it you know.

Policewoman   I'll be right outside.

She starts to go.

Janet   You don't know what it's been like. Your life's normal. We come from a different world.

Cross-fade to Scene Six.

Scene Six

Police interview room.

Susan *is interviewed by a female* **Police Inspector**.

Police Inspector   I'm just trying to imagine what led you to do it Susan.

Susan   He was fitting. We shot him.

Police Inspector   What did he do to you?

Susan   Nothing.

Police Inspector   How old are you Susan?

Susan   Thirty-six.

Police Inspector   Ever had a boyfriend?

Susan   No.

Police Inspector   What about your sister?

Susan   No.

Police Inspector   Never?

Susan   We were very close as a family. We didn't need that sort of thing.

Police Inspector   Most girls have boyfriends at some stage in their lives.

Susan   I know that.

Police Inspector   So why not you?

Silence.

Susan   We . . . had each other.

Police Inspector   Did he knock you about?

Pause.

Susan   Sometimes.

Police Inspector   Your mother? Your sister?

Susan   Sometimes.

Police Inspector   Badly?

Susan   He had . . . quite a temper. Sometimes.

Police Inspector   What got him in a temper?

Pause.

Susan   Things.

Police Inspector   Such as?

Pause.

Susan   We weren't to make a noise when we clicked on the light switch. (*Pause.*) Plates clattering. That wasn't allowed. (*Pause.*) Sometimes we buttered his toast wrong.

Police Inspector   Sometimes you buttered his toast wrong?

Susan   In the wrong direction. The butter in the wrong direction.

Police Inspector   I see . . .

Susan   You don't. You're just saying that. How could you see . . . you couldn't begin.

Police Inspector   Tell me then. Explain. Then maybe I will see.

Susan   I'm tired. I'm very tired. Don't ask me anything else, I just want to sleep now. I just want to sleep for a very long time. I think I'm coming down with something.

Police Inspector   You haven't told me everything Susan.

Susan   I'm sorry. I'm tired. I'm not well.

Pause.

Police Inspector   Did he sleep with you?

Susan   What? I think I've got a temperature, I'm burning. My face is burning. Is the floor tilting?

Police Inspector   Did he do anything sexual to you?

Susan   I'm sorry, you must think I'm drunk. Is it me or is it the room skewed like this? My head's in flames. I need aspirins. I need a doctor. I'm coming down with something.

Police Inspector   Your sister's told us he did.

Pause.

She told us he slept with both of you.

Susan   Oh. Oh.

Billy (*Narrative 2*)   Gather your thoughts, say nothing, take your time, there's still time. Don't say a word unless it's no. Laugh at her. Go on. Laugh. She's a bloody liar that Janet. Tell her she's mental.

Susan   I've a dry mouth.

Police Inspector   He did, didn't he? All your life since you were thirteen years old.

Silence.

Susan (*very quiet, cracked voice*)   Yes . . .

Billy (*Narrative 2*)   You bloody bitch, you did it. You've done it now. You said the thing that should never be said. Plaster cracking, the mould breaking, you're crumbling. You stand up but your legs buckle, snatch the yes back, take it back, go on. Shout no no, I didn't mean that. You're opening your mouth, go on, speak. There's rubble in your throat, ignore it. Just shout no, you stupid bitch, don't listen to the things crashing in your head. Hold yourself together, I'm shouting at you but you're not listening, I warned you, I bloody warned you, never bloody tell!

(*Narrative 1*)   And now a rush of fear unties her bladder, they've tricked her, she knows I'm not dead, not dead at all, and soon I'll burst through the window and kill her. Water splashing down her leg. Her eyes streaming. The dam is breached, the walls have collapsed. Get up off the floor you stupid bitch. Get up off the floor.

Scene Seven

Police interview room.

Mary   For two or three months they said we'll have to shoot him. I didn't think they meant it. But it was him or us. He was going down and he was taking us with him. We were frightened. We thought, one day he'll kill us and then shoot himself. And no one will ever know what went on. It's a form of torture to think that no one will ever know, isn't it?

Cross-fade to Scene Eight.

Scene Eight

Lawyer's office.

The interview has the quality of a dream in that the voice of the female **Lawyer** *seems to come from some distance away. We are firmly locked inside* **Janet**'*s head. Dialogue between* ● *and* ● *overlaps.*

Lawyer   ● We're trying to prepare a case for the defence –

Janet   I had clinical depression. That's what they called it. The doctor's kept saying why Janet, why are you like this?

Lawyer   – so if you can tell us everything you can about what happened, –

Janet   Every morning wake up crying I couldn't get out of the tunnel. It made him mad, he wanted me to smile, go on, take that look off your face, smile Janet, smile, or people might suspect.

Lawyer   – I think we may be able to provide a very strong case –

Janet   I couldn't do it any more, the muscles in my face stopped functioning.

Lawyer   – for citing mitigation, over a period of years –

Janet   – I just wanted whiskey and tablets and sleep. He'd shout you lot've got everything, you want for nothing.

Lawyer   Perhaps you'd like a cup of tea – ●

Janet   Every time I went to the hospital, every time I went to the doctor's, is there something you want to tell us? No, nothing, no. Because what could I say? Where would I start? And if I did, I knew he'd kill us all. Mum, then Susan, then me. In that order. Then himself. I knew he would because he told me.

Silence.

Lawyer   What did you feel when you'd shot him?

Janet   Pardon me?

Lawyer   When you shot him what were your feelings?

Janet   What did you feel here, what did you feel there, where did the intercourse take place? What difference does it make? The pictures in my head are mine and giving them to you won't wipe them out . . .

Lawyer   Janet! Are you listening?

Janet   I felt nothing.

Lawyer   You must have felt something.

Janet   No, I don't remember. We drank a lot of whiskey.

Lawyer   Did you feel relieved, elated?

Janet   You think he's gone now he's dead. But the dead don't go anywhere, they dance in your head, they come to you at night. The dead don't die. I know that now.

Lawyer   Did you love him?

Janet   Of course we did. He was our father.

Scene Nine

Police interview room.

Mary   I love you he said. Practically straight away. I believed him. I was twenty. I knew nothing. I was lonely and he was handsome.

Pause.

You don't understand do you? Neither do I.

Scene Ten

Billy (*Narrative 1*)   I don't remember pain, I don't remember pleasure. I was born aged six with teeth and a black, black heart. I'm what, eight? She has a new man now, a soft milky thing, no match for my lost blind dad. He winds wool for her with his limp fish hands. A voice like gruel. Boneless he is. And yet. And yet . . .

(*Narrative 2*)   Dark, feet like blocks of ice, heart bumping against my throat. Voices, burbling in the blackness, Is anybody there? Is anybody there? They got a drowned man once he spoke with weeds tangled in his throat I heard him. He opens his mouth and it's not that milky voice comes out of him it's dead people. Not frightened, me, I'm just cold that's what that banging noise is in my chest, cramp in my leg. Dry tongue. Stupid bastards don't know I'm here. Stupid bastards. There's someone coming through, he says there's someone coming through, it's a man. Stupid bastards I don't believe them I wish someone would put the light on, the skin's going tight on my head I think I'm having a heart attack – MAM! Billy? Is that you, let me stay, I want to stay, I won't make no noise. I told you, bloody bugger, I told you. She's pulling me, dragging me up the stairs, I'm fighting back, bloody get off me, bloody get off. No don't shut me up in the dark, it's black in there, the black gets in my mouth and nose and eyes I can't breathe. She says get in the cupboard and don't move you'll have no light, you don't deserve it. Bloody bugger bastard, I shout, bloody damn bugger. Crack. She hits me. Crack.

(*Narrative 1*)   I punch her hard, hard in the warm softness of her belly and she hugs me tight in her fierce arms. Billy love, Billy she says and she smiles. That's it Billy, that's it, keep your fury you'll need it out there. But never cry or I'll send the devil to you.

(*Narrative 2*)   No, no. I won't cry, don't send him, I don't want to see him, don't shut the door what if he comes Mam, what if he comes?

Door slamming, **Billy** *kicking.*

I won't cry. I bloody won't. Bastards . . . bloody damn blast shit bastards . . . don't send the devil to me . . . I don't want to see him . . . bloody bugger pig devils, I bloody am not I bloody am not I bloody am not frightened you buggers . . . you pig buggers.

Scene Eleven

Remand centre.

Susan and Janet (*together*)   Dear Mum, we are in a lovely
place with gardens and a small pond with fish, and it is
beautiful here. Last night we had baths with as much water
as we wanted and it was as close to heaven as we've ever
been. Everyone is kind, and our rooms are warm, people say
the rules are strict but we just laugh, Janet and me.
Sometimes we talk to lawyers. They are very nice. This is the
first time we've been free in the whole of our lives which is
funny really when you think about it because a remand
centre is actually a sort of prison isn't it? Thinking of you
often, your loving daughters, Susan and Janet.

Scene Twelve

Psychiatrist's office.

Psychiatrist   Are you sleeping now, Mary?

Mary   In the night he comes back to accuse me.

Psychiatrist   Of what?

Mary   Betrayal. He says, you let them kill me, and now I'll
have to kill you.

Psychiatrist   He can't harm you any more.

Mary   You don't get it.

Psychiatrist   Explain it to me, can you?

Mary   He'll never leave, it'll never be over, it'll never end.
I look at my legs, my arms, I look at my stomach, and he's
there. Scars. That was the time he did this or that, here is
where he broke my fingers. When I look in the mirror he's
there. When he comes into my dreams I think my heart will
stop. That's how he'll kill me. That's how he'll get me. I'll die
of fright.

Scene Thirteen

Billy (*Narrative 1*)   Our town is full of soldiers. There's a
war on. I like the shine on their boots, I like the sound they
make on the cobbles, harsh and strong, it sets my teeth
tingling. They are polished and trim and neat these men,
belted and tucked and ready for action, already I'm hooked.
I follow them to their barracks, oh the neatness of it, the rows
of bunks, the order, I'm beside myself with longing. Each bed
tight made, corners neat and parcelled, no gaps, no mistakes,
there's method in this. The air smells of carbolic and boot
polish and engine grease. One of them shows me his kit, his
boots gleaming under his bunk, placed just so, at just such an
angle, the precision of it makes me feel faint and then a
quivery ripple shivers across my groin. I am at home here. I
am in paradise here. The steel segs in my boots clash and
clatter on the hard floor. They take me to show me the
storerooms. Miles of shelving, stacked to the roof with
supplies. I say the word under my breath. Supplies. In case
of. In the event of. Supplies. This is organization. Nothing
can go wrong here. Everything, every last thing, labelled,
everything in its place. The soldier talks to me in his strange
accent, London or Scotland or somewhere, says you have to
be organized see, have to know where things are, because if
anything's out of place, if ever there's an emergency, think of
the chaos then. He shows me the order books, the chitties,
requisition pads, cancellation forms, goods in, goods out,
pink for in green for out, and things are dancing inside my
head, I'm practically singing. He lets me hold his gun. I
imagine shooting all the people in our street, pop, pop, pop. I
shoot them because they shouldn't be in here, messing
everything up, throwing the system into disarray. I imagine
the look on their faces, stupid, caught by surprise. Pop.
Astonishment, pain, fear, twisted mouths, some of them even
cry. I am laughing, shivers run up and down my spine, my
feet are going like Fred Astaire. I feel the most pleasure I've
ever felt. There, I think, there. See what it feels like. The
soldier takes the gun back. There's no bullets in it anyway.

Scene Fourteen

Psychiatrist's office.

Mary   When I met him he was gentle. Walked me to my door. Said you're the one for me. Said he'd known straight away. I wish I had a lad like that they all said. Polite and quiet and handsome. But I didn't like his mother, she said if you marry our Billy he'll put you through the eye of a needle. I didn't know what she meant. I do now. I was soft and shy, not the sort to argue. I was tiny. I was lonely. I was a bit of a wallflower. He must have seen me coming.

Scene Fifteen

Fifties dance hall music in background.

Billy (*Narrative 2*)   Tarts. Primping and powdering and giving you the eye, wouldn't mind if they meant it but no half the time they'd hardly give you a feel not that I'd want one. Not that I'd want one. Other fish to fry, me. They don't know, see. They can't see the rays coming off me. No idea, any of them. Look right through me because they don't know what they're dealing with I'd wipe the smiles off their faces I'd knock their bloody blocks off I'd have them on their knees begging they'd be. On their backs, begging –

(*Narrative 1*)   I'm tanked up, a bursting thing, I can feel the blood pounding in my head. I'm thinking how when I get like this I do things. Dark, jittery things. I'm thinking how I killed next door's cat to see how it felt. Better, I felt better for a while, seeing it squirm and cry, it was better than feeling up one of those tarts. There's a look I like to see, fear, is it, face twists, mouth pleads. I fizz and burn, my insides leap. Then after, nothing, dead is what I feel. It reminds me of something. I can't remember what. I'm just thinking this when I see her. Sitting quiet like a rabbit, none of the lipstick, none of the flash. She looks up at me. I know I'll marry her. This is the woman. This is the woman. This is the one. I see

my life mapped out before me, I see her, I see children, I see a
world. In a flash it comes together. I'm a pioneer. I'm in
enemy territory, I'm going to knock it into shape, impose a
bit of order. I'm going to carve out something for myself. I
dance in my heart. The world is a terrible place and this
woman will save me from it. The world is black and cold but
I'm taking her with me. She smiles. I feel like I did in the
army barracks. It's better than killing the cat. Although
somehow that's muddled in with it too.

Scene Sixteen

Psychiatrist's office.

Psychiatrist   You could have left him.

Mary   I did once. I went to my mother's. Took the girls
and ran. When we got there she wasn't in. When he came for
me there was no one to save us. Mary love. Don't be daft.
Come on home. I'm taking you home. Let's make it up. Give
me a kiss, come on. And there was a bit of the old Billy there,
the one I loved and I wanted to believe him so I went home
with him. When we got in the door he broke my ribs. Jumped
on them. I never went again. He said if we did he'd find us
and kill us.

Scene Seventeen

Psychiatrist's office.

Susan *talks to a female* **Psychiatrist**.

Psychiatrist 2   You must feel very angry Susan?

Susan   Pardon me?

Psychiatrist 2   With your mother. She let it happen all
those years.

Susan   They said we could go home now. They said unconditional bail.

Psychiatrist 2   Your mother was there all the time, and she did nothing to stop it, did she?

Susan   We don't think of it like that.

Psychiatrist 2   Why?

Susan   Why what?

Psychiatrist 2   D'you sometimes feel resentful towards her perhaps?

Susan   Why?

Psychiatrist 2   Why do you think?

Susan   We love her. She's our mum. Why d'you want us to be angry?

Psychiatrist 2   I wonder if sometimes you deny what it is you feel. It think it's understandable.

Susan   I think we live on different planets.

Pause.

I'm sorry, that was rude.

Psychiatrist 2   You must be rude if that's how you feel.

Susan   Most of what you say we don't understand.

Psychiatrist 2   You said yesterday you didn't mind going to prison. Do you mean that?

Susan   We killed him. He's dead. We feel better now. There's nothing you can do about any of it.

Psychiatrist 2   Let us try.

Pause.

Susan   This getting angry, this feeling this and feeling that. It's not for us. It's not really our sort of thing. It's too late now. You think you can understand but you can't see the size of it. If you had to live inside our heads for five minutes, you'd go mad and die. Best we deal with it ourselves.

Scene Eighteen

Remand centre. Bedroom.

Janet   I can't sleep Mum, I can't sleep on my own the bed's too big there are noises in the room, things creak, footsteps on the stairs, out in the corridor, I think it's him, every time I think it's him. They say he's dead but what if he's not? The golden glow's gone. Euphoria, they said, hysteria. Small dreams I had then, a glimpse of him, a hand here, a breath there, but quick to go. He's shrinking I thought, death has shrivelled him, soon he'll be gone. He's back now, the whole of him, his breath on my face, his hands in my hair, pulling me to places I want to forget. I'm not strong like Susan, soon I will die of this. Smile he says, smile. Big dreams now, huge dreams, no point in sleeping, there's no rest in it, no ease. Close my eyes and I'm trapped in the film of our life. Snap. Another photo. Snap. Smile Janet, smile. What will they make of these happy family snaps, our sandals and frocks, our arms entwined, a rabbit eating grass at our feet. And we're smiling smiling smiling smiling for our lives but at the back of my head I say please someone read this secret sign, I'm sending you a message read it read it please. This is not real this is not true, can't you see it in my eye. He kicks us where it can't be seen, under our hair, under our clothes, he boots us across the room. I want to tear off my dress and shout look look look look look. I look at the photo and where is the message, the sign in my eye? I look at the photo and we're just smiling.

Scene Nineteen

Family home.

Mary *is showing defence* **Lawyer** *round. As they move from room to room, a* **Photographer** *takes photos.*

Mary   This is where we slept. Billy and I. He had the bed by the window.

A camera flash whirs.

Lawyer 2   You slept in the living-room?

Mary   He was frightened of upstairs. All his life. Never slept up there.

Lawyer 2   Is this the. . . ?

Mary   That's where he died, yes. Lying on the bed. He did look peaceful. You'd never think to look at him he'd been shot.

Another photo.

Lawyer 2   What's this?

Mary   Medication list.

Lawyer 2 (*reading*)   'Dad: 4 Phenytion, 1 Sun, 1 Royal jelly, 1 vitamin. Mum: 1 Sun, 1 Royal jelly, 1 vitamin, 1 blood pressure, 1 Anti-Sickness . . .'

Mary   So there wouldn't be any mistakes.

Lawyer 2 (*handing it to junior*)   Put it in the file.

Mary   He liked things down on paper. Always best to have it in writing.

Lawyer 2   Did you put other things in writing?

Mary   Oh yes.

Lawyer 2   What?

Mary   Oh, most things really. Because you see if we didn't, there was always a risk, he said.

Lawyer 2   Of what?

Mary   That something might go wrong. Would you like to see upstairs?

Scene Twenty

Billy (*Narrative 2*)   I love my family. They're mine. I love them. What's different about me, see, is that I love them more than what you might call normal. Don't you ever say I don't love them because I do. I do. I've everything I want. A wife. Two girls. Glad they're girls. Nice balance. Nice sense of proportion. Me and them. Them and me. No one else. We don't need it. We don't want it. The house shipshape, it's all under control. Lay my hand on anything any time I want it. Blindfold.

Scene Twenty-one

Family home.

Cross-fade to **Mary** *showing the* **Lawyers** *and* **Photographer** *upstairs.*

Mary   And this is the other bedroom. The store room. (*She opens the door.*) The one we use for spare items.

They all pile in.

Billy did the shelving himself. It took him three weeks.

A photo is taken.

Scene Twenty-two

Cross-fade back to **Billy**.

Billy (*Narrative 2*)   I've got rules, I've got a system. What I say goes. Trained them so they know that. Glasses! Five inches from edge of table. Spoons! Bowl down when you drain them. That blue china cat, I like that cat. Three inches from fruit bowl. Not two not four but three. What I say goes. Got my eye on everything, got my ear to the ground. You can't take a breath without me. Don't even try.

Scene Twenty-three

Family home.

Cross-fade back to **Mary**.

Mary   It's arranged alphabetically d'you see? Brown polish, budgie food, bullets spare, bullets spent, curtain rings, dried peas and beans, pulses are in separate section under 'p', emergency supplies electrical only, firelighters –

Photos being taken.

Lawyer 2   You don't have any open fires.

Mary   No. They were just in case.

Lawyer 2   Of what?

Mary   He liked to cover all eventualities.

Scene Twenty-four

Cross-fade back to **Billy**.

Billy (*Narrative 2*)   Can't take any chances, can't take any risks. I'm the one that deals with it, I'm the one to face the bloody world. Earn a living. Put food in their mouths. They'd eat for England if I didn't stop them. Rations. Got them on rations. Like in the war. It's all there in writing. There's no excuse. Two ounces of this one ounce of that, three ounces only of the other. Keep a little edge of hunger there, keep them on their toes. I'm the one needs feeding up, I'm the one has to go out there. In the cold, in the dark, there's all sorts of stuff. Out in the real world. You've no idea. You don't know what it's like. You don't know nothing, you don't know you're born.

Scene Twenty-five

Family home.

Cross-fade back to **Mary**.

Mary   He made the rules. Each item to be no more than five inches apart and no less than two.

Lawyer 2   What happened if you got it wrong?

Mary   Sometimes a broken nose. Sometimes he just went into the shed and chopped up bones for soup. You could never tell. So we tried never to make mistakes. Which is quite difficult when the rules keep changing. It's quite tiring really.

Lawyer 2 (*reading as he walks round the room*)   'Garden implements, handkerchiefs (paper), hand cream, knives, macaroni, dried milk, pest poison, razor blades, rope, sugar, sticking plaster, tranquilizers, wrench, wire cutters, wool (darning), wool (knitting), water.'

Mary   Susan and Janet did the labels. They've a very neat hand haven't they?

More photos. The **Lawyer** *is bewildered.*

Lawyer 2   Did he ever explain the purpose of all this?

Mary   It's just spare items.

Lawyer 2   In case of what?

Mary   In case. That's all he said.

Lawyer 2   Didn't he ever say? Didn't you ever ask?

Mary   He was expecting a siege. Or a war. An explosion of some sort. He wanted to make sure that we'd survive, we'd be the only ones left. He wanted there to be just the four of us. He made us do the football pools. He said if we won, he'd buy a desert island miles from anywhere, and we'd all go and live there and never come back. That was his dream. It was our nightmare. We must have been the only family in England praying not to win.

Scene Twenty-six

Lawyer's office.

Susan *talks to the female* **Lawyer**.

Lawyer   It's not enough Susan. You have to tell us everything. We're trying to construct a defence.

Susan   I've told you.

Lawyer   When did he first start having intercourse with you?

Susan   I can't remember. I was quite young. Sixteen.

Lawyer   Yesterday you said thirteen.

Susan   It was a long time ago. I can't remember.

Lawyer   Sixteen or thirteen, which?

Susan   I was probably younger than sixteen. I don't know. Maybe I was thirteen.

Lawyer   And how did it happen?

Susan   Pardon me?

Lawyer   What were the events which led up to it?

Susan   He just said. He just said. You know.

Pause.

Lawyer   What?

Susan   I was in the shed. He was chopping bones. And he just. You know.

Lawyer   In the shed?

Susan   Pardon me?

Lawyer   It happened in the shed?

Susan   No. He told me in the shed.

Lawyer   Told you what?

Pause.

Susan   He said Susan you know I have sex with your mother well now I want it with you too.

Lawyer   And what did you say?

Susan   I just . . . I wasn't . . . I didn't know what it was. I knew it was bad.

Pause.

Could I have a glass of water please?

Water being poured. **Susan** *drinks.*

So I just said I don't want to Dad, I think it's wrong. And he said what he always said which is what I say goes.

Lawyer   And?

Susan   And what?

Lawyer   What happened then?

Susan   I waited. Nothing happened for a couple of weeks. I felt sick. I didn't know what was going to happen. I didn't know what to expect. One day he sent Mum and Janet out to a jumble sale. And that's when he did it.

Lawyer   Did you tell your mother?

Susan   I told her the day he said it in the shed.

Lawyer   And she did nothing?

Susan   She said it was bad enough the beatings without that as well.

Lawyer   But basically she did nothing.

Susan   There was nothing she could do. He'd bought a gun.

Lawyer   Did it happen regularly?

Susan   Every Friday. Other times in between.

Pause.

We were trapped. Stop looking at me like that. You don't understand. There was nothing we could do. He could have done it to you. Even someone like you. It's easy. You don't

fight. You don't know how to. You keep going. You
survive.

Pause.

You think we're freaks, don't you?

Lawyer   No.

Susan   Your mother couldn't have saved you either.
You're all in it together. You're all locked up together. And
you don't tell anyone . . . because it's . . . because it's
private.

Lawyer   Would you like a cup of tea?

Susan   I'm sorry for shouting.

Lawyer   You weren't shouting.

Susan   I'm sorry. Can I stop now?

Scene Twenty-seven

Remand centre.

Janet   Dear Dad, I'm writing this because the
psychiatrist says I should. I'm to tell you what I feel.
They ask us all the time. How does this make you feel
how does that make you feel what did you feel at this
time what did you feel at that? We know how to do it
now. We say what they want. We felt vulnerable, we felt
frightened, we felt terrified. What I feel is embarrassed.
Words words words. Useless every one. You were our
father and we killed you. We're glad you're dead but sad
you weren't nicer because then we wouldn't have had to
shoot you. Once when I was seven or eight, I came in
and you were at the sink playing with our goldfish you'd
tipped from its bowl. You were watching it flap and gasp
with a strange dreamy look in your eye. No colour in
them, all black. The corners of your mouth turned up.
That's how you looked after you'd hit Mum. That's all I
know about you. That look. I can't write this any more.

I don't understand the point. I don't think any of them really know what went on. We tell them this bit and that bit, but for them it's just some horrible incidents. A case history. Sometimes I think we'll never be free of you. Sometimes I want to come into your grave and shoot you again. And again and again and again. Just to make sure.

Scene Twenty-eight

Psychiatrist's office.

Susan *talks to the female* **Psychiatrist**.

Susan   Is there a drug you can get to stop you dreaming?

Psychiatrist 2   Why?

Susan   I'd like some.

Psychiatrist 2   What are your dreams about?

Pause.

Susan   Stuff. Is there a drug, then? Tablets or something?

Psychiatrist 2   Dreams are important.

Susan   They're not. They're just rubbish.

Psychiatrist 2   Sometimes dreams tell us how we really feel.

Susan   That's not true.

Psychiatrist 2   Tell me about them.

Pause. **Susan** *squirms.*

Susan   I can't.

Psychiatrist 2   Why can't you? Do they make you feel violent? Angry?

Susan   No.

Psychiatrist 2   What then?

Susan   I wish I'd never said it now.

Psychiatrist 2   You'd like the dreams to stop?

Susan   They're killing me. I can't live with them.

Psychiatrist 2   Try and tell me about them.

Long pause.

Susan   I dream that . . . I can't say it. I'm sorry.

Psychiatrist 2   Could you write it?

Susan   I can't say it. I can't write it. I can't get rid of it. I'm burning up with it.

Psychiatrist 2   With what?

Susan *begins to cry, in a dry, choked, reluctant way.*

Psychiatrist 2   If you tell me, I'll help you carry it. I won't be shocked.

Susan   I can never tell the worst. I can never tell.

Pause.

Psychiatrist 2   Is your father in these dreams?

Susan   Of course he is.

Psychiatrist 2   And what is he doing?

Susan*'s sobs burst from her.*

Susan   I can't tell you . . .

Psychiatrist 2   You can, you know.

Pause.

Susan   He's having sex with me. He's having sex with me and I'm . . . I'm . . .

She breaks off, sobbing. **Psychiatrist** *waits for a while.*

Psychiatrist 2   And you're what?

Susan   I'm enjoying it.

Scene Twenty-nine

Remand centre.

Susan   She said try writing it so I'm writing it. You come into the room. I can't see your face. It's dark. I'm lying on the bed and I've no clothes on. You kiss me a lover's kiss. You put your tongue inside my mouth and you tell me that you love me. I say I love you too. That's what lovers say isn't it. I love you too. Dad. I say I love you too Dad. I can't write this. She said the dreams will fade if I write it down. She says it's normal. These feelings are normal. I say they're not my feelings they're my dreams. You touch me. I want you to. It's you and it's not you. I ask you to touch me again. And you do. You keep telling me you love me. I look at your face above me, and you look so sad, and I'm not your daughter I'm your lover. Except I'm lying now because I know I'm your daughter and that's what makes it so special, and secret. You look so sad but I will make everything better for you. I don't want you to stop. You're the only lover I've ever had. I pull you down towards me. I wake up. I'm sick over the side of the bed. How could you do this to me Dad? How could you do this?

Scene Thirty

Mary *is visiting* **Susan** *and* **Janet**.

Susan   We can come home next week.

Janet   Until the trial.

Mary   That's very kind of them.

Susan   We're not a danger to society.

Mary   Of course you're not.

Janet   Or to ourselves. That's what they said.

Susan   We can all be together again.

Mary   That'll be nice.

Susan   We won't be staying in the house.

Janet   They're going to put us somewhere else.

Susan   Without bad memories.

Janet   A nice flat they said.

Mary   I dreamt he came back and tore the curtains down then pulled the house down around us, pulled the walls down, the ceilings, bricks and dust and plaster everywhere. We were choking and suffocating. There was plaster in our mouths. Then I woke up. I thought, I think I'd like to live somewhere else. Somewhere I might get some sleep.

Susan   They've given Janet a tape.

Janet   A relaxation tape. I listen to it on a Walkman.

Mary   Does it help?

Janet   No.

Susan   She's not doing it right.

Janet   You have to concentrate. He keeps getting in the way.

Mary   It'll be better when we're all together.

Janet   I'll sleep in your bed.

Mary   Yes.

Janet   Until the dreams stop.

Susan   What's it like without him Mum?

Mary   I had mushrooms on toast yesterday. I haven't had that since I was a girl.

Susan   We went shopping yesterday. With Deirdre.

Janet   She's one of the staff.

Mary   Very kind.

Janet   We didn't know what to buy.

Susan   We felt a bit light-headed.

Janet   We felt a bit sick.

Susan   It was a hypermarket. We had five pounds each.

Janet   We bought some Shredded Wheat.

Susan   And three packets of biscuits.

Janet   Deidre laughed. She said is that all you want?

Susan   But we'd never had Shredded Wheat.

Janet   We'd seen it on the telly.

Susan   She said you two are weird.

Janet   They weren't very nice actually. The Shredded Wheat. But I expect we'll get used to them.

Scene Thirty-one

Billy (*Narrative 1*)   It's my home I do as I like. The girls are grown now. The girls are dangerous. I've got them taped I've got them tabbed, don't let them out of my sight. Dress them the same, them and their mother, three red jackets so I can see them coming. My little army, my little crew. There's men on the streets, men on the corners. I've seen them, I know what they want.

(*Narrative 2*)   Right I say right, no talking to men no talking to boys not now not ever d'you hear me. Point my gun that always gets them, never argue with a gun I taught them that. Oh yes Dad no Dad three bags full Dad but they're bloody lying just like their mother, say one thing mean another, don't know why they bother I know everything. If you go with other men I'll bloody kill you, oh we don't Dad we don't, oh butter wouldn't melt but I know women I know you, you say one word, you flash one look, we don't Dad, we don't, but they're taking the piss. This is what I'll do this is what I'll do, bang bang bang!

(*Narrative 1*)   I fire at the wall and they jump and cower, so I do it again, I'm tingling and racing, there's holes in the wall. I fire at their feet to make them dance, oh I'm laughing now, and then she spoils it, she bloody spoils it. She starts to cry. So I punch her hard but she still keeps going.

(*Narrative 2*)   I've told you, I've told you, no bloody tears in this house, no bloody tears. She keeps on, she keeps on, I want her out of here, get her out, before the room explodes. Move, bloody move, what's wrong with you?

(*Narrative 1*)   She doesn't go. So I do, I go. I lie in the garden, face down in the wet grass, gun sleeping soft beside me. Rain patters and splashes around me. I could sleep for a year. I wish I was dead. I don't know why but I do.

Scene Thirty-two

Remand centre.

Susan   He bought us rings.

Janet   Wedding rings.

Susan   We went to the jewellers and chose them ourselves.

Janet   Mine was patterned.

Susan   Mine was plain.

Janet   The jeweller was delighted, he said to Dad –

Susan   – oh, a double wedding –

Janet   And Dad said –

Billy   Yes.

Susan   In his special voice. His outside voice.

Janet   Polite and reasonable. Normal.

Billy   Yes. They'll both be wives.

Janet   And we put on our rings when we left the shop.

Susan   He said it was to keep us safe.

Janet   To keep the men at bay.

Susan   He wasn't a bad man.

Janet   In his own way.

Susan   But he needed to be put down.

Janet   The way you do with dogs.

Susan   You put them out of their misery.

Janet   Sometimes he'd lie on the floor and shout.

Billy   I don't want to live. I want out, I want out.

Susan   So really we did him a favour.

Janet   Either he went or we all did.

Susan   It was just a matter of time.

Janet   We used to imagine the headlines.

Susan   Family found dead in Burnley.

Janet   He wouldn't let us leave.

Susan   We couldn't let him live. (*Interior*.) Sometimes he
kissed me in the street, not a father's kiss. And that's when I
began to think we were invisible. People were nearby, people
we knew, and nobody said a word. We'd slipped into another
world where nobody spoke. No one said nothing. Janet, me,
Mum, Dad. And no one else did either. But they knew, they
saw. All that silence. Five kinds of silence. Each of ours and
the world outside. Cars went by, people out shopping, drinks
were bought in pubs, and we slipped through it all like
ghosts. This man is my father I wanted to shout. But either
they knew and they didn't care or they didn't know because
they couldn't see. I was banging on the glass but it made no
noise, I was opening my mouth but no voice came. He was
turning us into ghosts, sucking away at our lives, soon we'd
be gone, and the dust would settle. As if we'd never been.
This most frightening of all: as if we'd never been. We felt the
waters closing over us. He was dragging us down to
unmourned graves, and with one last gasp we made for the
surface where we saw the light, threw ourselves on the mercy
of the air. One square of light. A promise of breathing
unaided, and we saw our chance in the darkness. There was
no option, do you see that? When you're drowning you

snatch at life. We came out of the dark and into the light. We are new-born babies and we're learning to walk.

Scene Thirty-three

Billy (*Narrative 1*)   I'm standing at the sink. Fizz, crack, there's a ripple in my head, a burning smell. My face in the mirror, mouth frozen open, no sound coming out. Fizz, crackle electric shocks through my brain, shattering it into fragments, hundreds and thousands of coloured glass. I am dissolving, the room turns magenta pink. When I come to I'm in bed. Epilepsy they say. Fits. Bring me my gun I shout and no one moves a muscle. They're sort of smiling and patting my hand. And then I realize I'm not actually talking. I'm not even moving my mouth. God damn you bastards and this last word like a roar burst from my lungs and smashes them in the face.

(*Narrative 2*)   Bastards! Oh you can hear me now all right. Let's get this place shipshape, I'm not out for the count yet. I'm getting up. No Billy, the doctor says – sod the bloody doctor, I hope he rots in hell, bring me my bloody gun. Janet sitting there snivelling, what's the matter with her, why can't she smile? Smile, Janet, smile, or I'll knock your bloody block off if anyone hears of what goes on in this house I'll shoot you all in the legs. I have not got bloody epilepsy. I bloody have not and if any of you says that word again I'll set the house on fire. It's banned right. I'll set the house on fire with all of us in it. Crack. A noise. Where did that come from? Is it outside or in my head? I say nothing. I don't let on. Bring me the gun, let's have a party, I'm feeling on top of the world. Tell her to stop crying, will you, tell her to shut her face. Let's all have a whiskey, let's get this show on the road.

(*Narrative 1*)   Crack. Someone's popping something in my head. Best say nothing. But they're looking at me like I'm an unusual fish or something.

(*Narrative 2*)   What's wrong with you, what are you gawping at? Someone bring me a sandwich. Move it. Go on move it. What's wrong, are you bloody deaf or something?

(*Narrative 1*)   When I come to, Mary's holding my hand and I'm on the floor. She says I've had a fit but she's just saying it. What I think is some bastard spiked my drink.

Scene Thirty-four

Remand centre.

Susan   The fits got worse.

Janet   They took him into hospital.

Susan   And that was the happiest time of our lives.

Janet   It was lovely to wake up every morning, knowing he wasn't there.

Susan   We could eat what we wanted.

Janet   Read magazines.

Susan   The bruises began to fade.

Janet   That's when we knew. We got a taste of forbidden fruit.

Susan   We understood what we didn't have. He was sunk from then on really.

Janet   And when he first came home he seemed different.

Susan   Weak as a kitten, quiet as a lamb.

Janet   We were walking on air.

Susan   But it didn't last.

Janet   The last weekend was like being in hell.

Scene Thirty-five

A TV quiz show tinkles merrily in the background.

Billy (*Narrative 1*)   The walls are closing in, I have to keep a hold of things, keep my ear to the ground. Doctors in and out of the place, something wrong with Janet. They want to put her in hospital. Mental hospital. Stupid bloody woman what's she got to cry about? It's driving me mad, the weeping, I can't bloody stand it. I've got a few worries, things preying on my mind, I don't like the sound of this mental home. If they take her there I want her drugged I don't want her talking I don't want her spilling the beans. Maybe I should shoot the lot of them now. Then me. No, not yet. There's life in the old dog yet.

(*Narrative 2*)   Another little whiskey. Everything's under control. More crackling in my head last night I didn't say a word. Give them an inch and they'll take a mile. A bird in the hand is worth two in the bush. What I say goes, what I say goes. Somebody come in here I'm on my own in the dark. Mary, Susan, Janet, somebody come and do something. Stop bloody crying, you live the life of Riley you don't want for nothing. I want a fried egg and I want Janet to make it. Do as you're bloody told, there's nothing wrong with you. Do as you're bloody told. If the yolk breaks you know what you get. Any sign of burning and you know what you get. And any more tears and I'll break your arms. Another little whiskey. Crack. Sparks fly. Bright phosphorescence. My brain hisses and fizzes. Crack. Oh. Oh. I am hurtling through black sky on a sea of pungent scent I can smell the colours of my own mind I can smell this television programme I'm back to my dog self, back to the dream. Metal, I smell metal and wood and cordite, Janet's tears, Susan's breasts, I smell something blinding white and relentless. I smell things I can't control. Piss, my piss, something between my teeth, bite on this Dad, bite on this, I can't go on says someone. Load the gun, oh, burning tyres, spent diesel, an overtone of brass, stinging nettles, cold sweat I love that smell so why don't I love it now. We'll have to shoot him, my body bucking, the room is

rank with it my eyes stream with it, my fear is filling the
room. Bang. Bang. Bang.

Scene Thirty-six

Susan and Janet (*together*)   When the judge told us we
weren't going to prison we wanted to say thank you but
nothing came out. She said you've suffered enough. That
was very kind of her we thought.

Susan   We can start a new life now.

Janet   We've got a maisonette.

Susan   We plan to have pink carpets.

Janet   And a dog.

Susan   We've got four bedrooms.

Janet   One for each of us.

Susan   And one for spare items.

Janet   We've already bought the shelving.

Music.